AF864755

Behavioralizing Finance

Behavioralizing Finance

Hersh Shefrin

Leavey School of Business
Santa Clara University
Santa Clara, CA 95053
USA
hshefrin@scu.edu

now

the essence of knowledge

Boston – Delft

Foundations and Trends® in Finance

Published, sold and distributed by:
now Publishers Inc.
PO Box 1024
Hanover, MA 02339
USA
Tel. +1-781-985-4510
www.nowpublishers.com
sales@nowpublishers.com

Outside North America:
now Publishers Inc.
PO Box 179
2600 AD Delft
The Netherlands
Tel. +31-6-51115274

The preferred citation for this publication is H. Shefrin, Behavioralizing Finance, Foundations and Trends® in Finance, vol 4, nos 1–2, pp 1–184, 2009

ISBN: 978-1-60198-330-5
© 2010 H. Shefrin

All rights reserved. No part of this publication may be reproduced, stored in a retrieval system, or transmitted in any form or by any means, mechanical, photocopying, recording or otherwise, without prior written permission of the publishers.

Photocopying. In the USA: This journal is registered at the Copyright Clearance Center, Inc., 222 Rosewood Drive, Danvers, MA 01923. Authorization to photocopy items for internal or personal use, or the internal or personal use of specific clients, is granted by now Publishers Inc for users registered with the Copyright Clearance Center (CCC). The 'services' for users can be found on the internet at: www.copyright.com

For those organizations that have been granted a photocopy license, a separate system of payment has been arranged. Authorization does not extend to other kinds of copying, such as that for general distribution, for advertising or promotional purposes, for creating new collective works, or for resale. In the rest of the world: Permission to photocopy must be obtained from the copyright owner. Please apply to now Publishers Inc., PO Box 1024, Hanover, MA 02339, USA; Tel. +1-781-871-0245; www.nowpublishers.com; sales@nowpublishers.com

now Publishers Inc. has an exclusive license to publish this material worldwide. Permission to use this content must be obtained from the copyright license holder. Please apply to now Publishers, PO Box 179, 2600 AD Delft, The Netherlands, www.nowpublishers.com; e-mail: sales@nowpublishers.com

Foundations and Trends® in Finance

Volume 4 Issues 1–2, 2009

Editorial Board

Editor-in-Chief:
George M. Constantinides
Leo Melamed Professor of Finance
The University of Chicago
Graduate School of Business
5807 South Woodlawn Avenue
Chicago IL 60637
USA
gmc@gsb.uchicago.edu

Editors

Franklin Allen
Nippon Life Professor of Finance and Economics,
The Wharton School, The University of Pennsylvania

Andrew W. Lo
Harris & Harris Group Professor, Sloan School of Management,
Massachusetts Institute of Technology

René M. Stulz
Everett D. Reese Chair of Banking and Monetary Economics,
Fisher College of Business, The Ohio State University

Editorial Scope

Foundations and Trends® in Finance will publish survey and tutorial articles in the following topics:

- Corporate Governance
- Corporate Financing
- Dividend Policy and Capital Structure
- Corporate Control
- Investment Policy
- Agency Theory and Information
- Market Microstructure
- Portfolio Theory
- Financial Intermediation
- Investment Banking
- Market Efficiency
- Security Issuance
- Anomalies and Behavioral Finance
- Asset-Pricing Theory
- Asset-Pricing Models
- Tax Effects
- Liquidity
- Equity Risk Premium
- Pricing Models and Volatility
- Fixed Income Securities
- Computational Finance
- Futures Markets and Hedging
- Financial Engineering
- Interest Rate Derivatives
- Credit Derivatives
- Financial Econometrics
- Estimating Volatilities and Correlations

Information for Librarians

Foundations and Trends® in Finance, 2009, Volume 4, 4 issues. ISSN paper version 1567-2395. ISSN online version 1567-2409. Also available as a combined paper and online subscription.

Foundations and Trends® in
Finance
Vol. 4, Nos. 1–2 (2009) 1–184
© 2010 H. Shefrin
DOI: 10.1561/0500000030

the essence of knowledge

Behavioralizing Finance

Hersh Shefrin

Mario L. Belotti Professor of Finance, Leavey School of Business, Santa Clara University, Santa Clara, CA 95053, USA hshefrin@scu.edu

Abstract

Finance is in the midst of a paradigm shift, from a neoclassical based framework to a psychologically based framework. Behavioral finance is the application of psychology to financial decision making and financial markets. Behavioralizing finance is the process of replacing neoclassical assumptions with behavioral counterparts. This monograph surveys the literature in behavioral finance, and identifies both its strengths and weaknesses. In doing so, it identifies possible directions for behavioralizing the frameworks used to study beliefs, preferences, portfolio selection, asset pricing, corporate finance, and financial market regulation. The intent is to provide a structured approach to behavioral finance in respect to underlying psychological concepts, formal framework, testable hypotheses, and empirical findings. A key theme of this monograph is that the future of finance will combine realistic assumptions from behavioral finance and rigorous analysis from neoclassical finance.

Contents

1

Introduction

Viewed as a field, behavioral finance is the application of psychology to financial decision making and financial markets. Viewed as a process, behavioral finance is about the transformation of the financial paradigm from a neoclassical based framework to a psychologically based framework. I refer to this process as "behavioralizing finance."

Neoclassical finance has both strengths and weaknesses. Among its main strengths is its systematic, rigorous framework. Among its main weaknesses is its reliance on the unrealistic assumption that all decision makers are fully rational. Behavioral finance also has both strengths and weaknesses. Among its main strengths is its use of assumptions based on findings from the psychology literature about how people deviate from fully rational behavior. Among its main weaknesses is the reliance by its proponents on an ad hoc collection of models that lack mutual consistency and a unifying structure.

In this monograph I suggest that finance is moving to a new paradigm that will combine structural features from neoclassical finance and realistic assumptions from behavioral finance. To develop this position, I describe the outlines of what such a synthesis entails, and relate it to the issues associated with structure, coherence, and consistency.

The behavioralization of finance involves intellectual shifts by two groups. The first shift features neoclassical economists explicitly incorporating psychological elements into their models. For a sense of neoclassical resistance, see Ross (2005). The second shift features behavioral economists developing a systematic, rigorous framework. For example, most of the current behavioral explanations for the cross-section of returns rely on models that feature a single risky security, rather than the cross-section itself. In addition, one well-known behavioral result might well be incorrect. The behavioral result contends that irrational investors can survive in the long run because they take on more risk than rational investors. However, this contention is at odds with theorems in the general literature about long-run survivability.

Shifts necessary for the behavioralization of finance are underway. Some neoclassical economists have begun to develop behavioral models. Two prominent examples are Jouini and Napp (2006) and Dumas et al. (2009). At the same time, some behavioral economists are beginning to develop models that are as rigorous as their neoclassical counterparts. A good example is Xiong and Yan (2009), whose formal framework shares much in common with Dumas et al. (2009).

These shifts are taking place against a historical backdrop in which financial economists from both camps have displayed some of the same psychological traits that are the focus of behavioral finance. Confirmation bias may well be at the top of the list, the tendency to overweight evidence that confirms one's views relative to evidence that disconfirms those views. My own experience has been that both neoclassical economists and behavioral economists have been resistant to the proposal that each needs to move to a common middle ground where psychological assumptions and rigor come together. Take for example, the behavioral pricing kernel framework, which is an approach I favor. For years, neoclassical economists have tended to claim that the behavioral pricing kernel theorems discussed in Section 5 of this monograph are wrong. However, this situation is changing slowly as some of these theorems have come to be replicated in the work of more traditional economists, such as Jouini and Napp (2006). Likewise, behavioral economists have resisted the unified, systematic approach, arguing that a sentiment-based pricing kernel framework is insufficiently behavioral.

In the past, both neoclassical and behavioral economists have chosen to exclude papers relating to the behavioral pricing kernel at their respective NBER meetings.

I write this survey as some neoclassical economists and behavioral economists have begun the process of moving toward a common middle ground. My approach to this monograph is to describe the highlights of the behavioral finance literature, as expressed through prior surveys, and to identify some of the weaknesses of this literature. These foundations are the subject of Section 2. In the remainder of the monograph, I have two main objectives. My first objective is to discuss works which have emerged since the past surveys appeared, or which those surveys overlooked for one reason or another. My second objective is to present some ideas about trends toward a unifying framework for behavioral finance which captures some of the rigor in neoclassical finance. The contents of these sections represent my thinking about the nature of the common middle ground which brings together the best of neoclassical finance and behavioral finance.

When it comes to asset pricing, the common middle ground involves models that identify how markets aggregate heterogeneous investors' beliefs. In some respects, some of the models employed by neoclassical economists are structurally similar to those employed by behavioral economists. Two neoclassical examples are Detemple and Murthy (1994) and Kurz (1997). A behavioral example is Shefrin and Statman (1994). Notably, the neoclassical assumptions involve rational behavior by all agents. For example, Kurz describes the agents in his framework as holding "rational beliefs." In contrast, the behavioral assumptions specify that the source of the heterogeneity is a series of heuristics that give rise to biased beliefs. The modelig distance between the two approaches is short. However, moving from the neoclassical position to the behavioral position requires a philosophical leap.

1.1 Brief History

Behavioral finance is relatively new as a subject of study. Although the *Journal of Finance* published the first formal paper in behavioral finance in 1972 (see Slovic (1972), financial economists did not begin to apply the concepts pioneered by Slovic and other psychologists working in behavioral decision making until the early 1980s. Even then, it took more than a decade for the behavioral approach to gain traction. The first published work in behavioral finance by economists was Shefrin and Statman (1984). In December 1984, the late Fischer Black, then President-elect of the American Finance Association, invited Meir Statman and me to organize the first behavioral session at the annual meetings. At the session Statman presented our paper on the disposition effect, Shefrin and Statman (1985), and De Bondt presented his work with Richard Thaler on overreaction, DeBondt and Thaler (1985). These two papers set the stage for two main streams in the behavioral finance literature, one pertaining to irrationality in investor behavior and the other to inefficiency in asset pricing.

Subsequently, Thaler organized a behavioral research group, first at the Sloan Foundation, and then later at the Sage Foundation, which ultimately led to the NBER Behavioral Finance program. In addition to De Bondt, Statman, Thaler, and myself, the main participants at the Sloan and Sage Foundation included Daniel Kahneman, Amos Tversky, Paul Andreassen, Robert Shiller, Fischer Black, Richard Roll, David Dreman, Larry Summers, and Andrei Shleifer. Thaler collected many of the papers written by members of this group into an edited collection: see Thaler (1993).

Despite the beginnings of a convergence that I mentioned above, currently there is a wide spectrum of views about behavioral finance. At one extreme you will still find the view expressed by some that behavioral finance is nothing more than a collection of findings about anomalies relative to the efficient market hypothesis. At the other extreme you will find the view that the behavioral approach already constitutes a coherent paradigm, with a systematic approach involving psychological concepts, a formal framework, testable hypotheses, and empirical findings. Between the extremes are views that acknowledge that behavioral finance possesses some structure and can be credited with some successes, but overall still lacks coherence and consistency.

In the last decade several surveys of behavioral finance have been written. Hirshleifer (2008a), Barberis and Thaler (2003), Subrahmanyam (2007), and De Bondt et al. (2008) survey the general area, while Baker et al. (2007b) survey behavioral corporate finance. There is little point in fully replicating what can already be found in those surveys. Instead, my intent in this monograph is to summarize the key features of those surveys, and relate these features to the process of behavioralizing finance.

1.2 Organization of Monograph: Foundations and Trends

I have organized this monograph to highlight both the strengths and weaknesses of the behavioral approach. Its strengths emanate from basing its foundations on a rich literature in psychology. Its weaknesses emanate from an overall approach that has been piecemeal. There is no generally accepted coherent behavioral counterparts to the workhorses of neoclassical finance, mean-variance portfolios, asset pricing theory, and the value maximizing agency theory approach to corporate finance. In contrast, much of the literature in behavioral finance is scattered, ad hoc, unsystematic, and lacking in discipline. In one sense the lack of discipline is a positive, as behavioral finance is new, and it might be a mistake to narrow its range of inquiry too early, thereby stifling major new insights. However, it seems to me that many proponents of behavioral finance have been excessively resistant to rigorous analysis, and the time has come to move in the direction of increased rigor and discipline.

Any discussion of paradigm transformation would be incomplete without addressing how behavioral assumptions will impact the major building blocks lying at the heart of the neoclassical framework. These are: mean-variance portfolios, the efficient market hypothesis, the capital asset pricing model, the Black–Scholes option pricing formula, and the Modigliani–Miller principle. This monograph will describe how the substitution of neoclassical assumptions with behavioral assumptions will impact these building blocks.

Section 2 highlights the foundations of behavioral finance by surveying a sequence of surveys. The remaining five sections focus on trends relating to a more rigorous approach to behavioral finance, or more broadly, the behavioralization of finance.

Chapters 2–8

Section 2 is a survey of recent surveys of behavioral finance. The section summarizes the major contributions to behavioral finance, as seen through the eyes of some of its key contributors. This discussion provides an overview of the field, and sets the stage for identifying both the strengths and weaknesses of the behavioral approach. The remaining sections provide an opportunity to present some thoughts on what a systematic behavioral approach might entail.

Section 3 introduces the key psychological concepts used in behavioral finance. These concepts divide naturally into beliefs and preferences, both of which reflect human psychology. Among the belief-related psychological concepts discussed in the section are unrealistic optimism, overconfidence, and representativeness. Among the preference-related concepts are prospect theory, SP/A theory, regret, and self-control.

Section 4 deals with behavioral portfolio selection. Beliefs pertain to the manner in which investors' judgments about risk and return reflect bias. Behavioral beliefs involve a series of biases such as hot hand fallacy, gambler's fallacy, and home bias. Preferences pertain to the manner in which investors frame and evaluate cash flow representations. Framing effects lead many investors to adopt a piecemeal approach to portfolio selection, in which purchasing decisions are influenced by salience or attention, and realization decisions are influenced by a phenomenon known as "the disposition effect." The disposition effect is the tendency to sell winners too early and ride losers too long in all months of the year except December. Behavioral preferences also explain how investors segment their portfolios into risk layers, and exhibit a taste for positive skewness. The section describes a series of hypotheses about the preference for dividend-paying stocks that stem from the behavioral finance literature, and describes findings from tests of these hypotheses.

Section 5 describes how behavioral portfolio choices impact asset pricing. The literature on behavioral asset pricing theory is eclectic, and features a wide variety of models, centered on the concept of sentiment. Many of the models in the behavioral asset pricing literature were developed to analyze overreaction and underreaction in financial markets. With the intent of describing a less eclectic, more systematic approach to asset pricing, the section focuses on a behavioral SDF-based approach. This approach brings together the powerful asset pricing tools favored by neoclassical asset pricing theorists and the realistic assumptions favored by behavioral asset pricing theorists. The behavioral SDF-based approach offers a unified treatment of behavioral beliefs and behavioral preferences, showing how these features combine to impact the mean-variance frontier, equity prices, the term structure of interest rates, and option prices. In this respect, the discussion in the section emphasizes the latter two applications.

Section 6 discusses behavioral corporate finance. Behavioral corporate finance is concerned with the manner in which behavioral beliefs, behavioral preferences, and inefficient prices impact the corporate financial decisions made by managers. The literature on behavioral corporate finance involves the study of how psychology impacts capital budgeting, capital structure, corporate governance, and mergers and acquisitions. In the section I focus on three themes that strike me as areas providing fertile ground for future work. The three areas are the study of how specific individual traits impact corporate financial decisions, the impact of group composition on collective corporate financial decisions and corporate value, and the manner in which psychological characteristics of entrepreneurs impact the choices they make about risk and return.

Section 7 discusses the role which psychological factors play in the structure of financial market regulation. The section points out the importance of psychological forces in the shaping of the major legislation underlying financial market regulation in the United States. Examples of past regulation are merit regulation ("blue sky laws"), the Securities Act of 1933, the Securities Exchange Act of 1934, Sarbanes–Oxley, and regulations covering the Savings & Loan industry. Issues which are more contemporary involve the regulation of financial derivatives, investment banks, ratings agencies, hedge funds, and the credit card industry. The section describes how capture theory, perceptions of fairness, and shocks to the economic and financial system impact the regulatory system, especially issues pertaining to the global financial crisis that erupted in 2008.

Section 8 contains some concluding remarks which highlight the main points in this monograph.

1.3 Home Bias and Omissions

As I mentioned above, Section 2 provides a survey of recent surveys, beginning with Hirshleifer (2008a) and moving on to Barberis and Thaler (2003), Baker et al. (2007b), and Subrahmanyam (2007). All of these surveys reflect the biases of their authors in terms of perspective and emphasis. Home bias is particularly evident, meaning authors are prone to emphasize their own work. No single survey is comprehensive. For example, none of these surveys discusses the experimental work on asset pricing bubbles, particularly the work of Smith: See his Nobel address, Smith (2003).

In the interest of disclosure about home bias and omissions, I should say at the outset that this survey will follow suit, meaning it will also feature home bias and omissions. Surveys are part review, part synthesis, and part editorial. I hold particular views about the state of behavioral finance, its strengths, its weaknesses, and quo vadis–where it is going? I plan to use this survey as a vehicle to communicate my perspective about the direction in which I would like to see behavioral finance specifically, and finance generally, go.

2

Survey of Surveys

This section describes the highlights of four surveys of behavioral finance that have appeared in the past decade. Because there is a fair amount of overlap in these surveys, I select portions of each to identify key concepts and trace the different perspectives.

I begin with the survey by Hirshleifer (2008a). Hirshleifer presents a thorough treatment of the underlying psychology upon which proponents of behavioral finance draw. He also discusses how many of these psychological concepts have been applied to asset pricing, and to a lesser extent corporate finance. I focus on Hirshleifer's review of the psychology and some of the broad issues in asset pricing.

I then present the highlights of a survey by Barberis and Thaler (2003). In discussing Barberis and Thaler's survey, I focus on their discussion of specific issues in asset pricing. For the discussion of corporate finance, I describe the highlights of the survey written by Baker et al. (2007b). Finally, I discuss the perspective of a more recent general survey by Subrahmanyam (2007).

Proponents of behavioral finance draw on a rich literature in psychology which documents phenomena that interfere with rational beliefs and decisions. The list includes overconfidence, unrealistic optimism, representativeness, conservatism, self-attribution bias, confirmation bias, anchoring, availability bias, loss aversion, aversion to a sure loss, and probability weighting. The last three phenomena are major features of prospect theory, a choice framework developed by Kahneman and Tversky (1979). All other phenomena are part of an approach known as heuristics and biases.

The volume edited by Kahneman et al. (1982) contains most of the foundation contributions to the heuristics and biases literature. A heuristic is a crude rule of thumb for making judgments about probabilities, statistics, future outcomes, etc. A bias is a predisposition toward making a particular judgmental error. The heuristics and biases approach studies the heuristics upon which people rely to form judgments, and the associated biases in those judgments.

Glossary of Biases

Some biases are associated with specific heuristics. Examples of these biases relate to such heuristic principles as availability, anchoring, and representativeness.

Availability is the tendency to form judgments based on information which is readily available, but to underweight information that is not readily available. For example, a person might underestimate the danger from riptides and overestimate the danger from shark attacks because the media tends to report most shark attacks but rarely reports less dramatic incidents involving riptides. Heuristics and biases associated with availability reflect the importance of salience and attention.

Anchoring is the tendency to formulate an estimate by using a process that begins with an initial number (the anchor) and then making adjustments relative to the anchor. Anchoring bias is the tendency for the associated adjustments to be too small.

Representativeness is the tendency to rely on stereotypes to make a judgment. For example, a person who relies on representativeness might be especially bold in predicting that the future return of a particular stock will be very favorable because its past long-term performance has been very favorable. This is because they form the judgment that favorable past performance is representative of good stocks. However, representativeness leads such predictions to be overly bold, because of insufficient attention to factors that induce regression to the mean.

Although some biases relate directly to specific heuristics, other biases stem from a variety of factors. For example, people tend to be overconfident about both their abilities and their knowledge. People who are overconfident about their abilities overestimate those abilities. People who are overconfident about their knowledge tend to think they know more than they actually do. In particular, people who are overconfident about their knowledge tend to establish excessively narrow confidence intervals. Such people end up being surprised at their mistakes more often than they had anticipated.

Other examples of biases that do not stem directly from specific heuristics are unrealistic optimism and the illusion of control. Unrealistic optimism involves overestimating the probabilities of favorable events and underestimating the probabilities of unfavorable events. The illusion of control is overestimating the role of skill relative to luck in the determination of outcomes.

Extrapolation bias leads people to overreact, developing unwarranted forecasts that recent changes will continue into the future. Confirmation bias leads people to overweight information which confirms their prior views, and to underweight information which disconfirms those views. Conservatism is the tendency to underreact by overweighting base rate information relative to new (or singular) information. The affect heuristic refers to basing judgments on feelings rather than on underlying fundamentals. Reliance on the affect heuristic is often described as "gut feeling" or intuition.

Hindsight bias is the tendency to view outcomes in hindsight as being more likely than warranted. That is, ex post the ex ante probability of the event that actually occurred is judged to be higher than the ex ante judgment of that ex ante probability.

Categorization is the act of partitioning objects into general categories and ignoring the differences among members of the same category. Categorization bias can be severe if the members of the same category are different from each other in meaningful ways.

Status quo bias predisposes people to favor inaction over action, perhaps because of regret aversion. See Samuelson and Zeckhauser (1988).

The discussion of prospect theory, which lies at the center of the psychological-based approach to choice, is deferred until later in this section and the section following.

2.1 Hirshleifer (2001): Review of Psychology Literature and Link to Asset Pricing

2.1.1 Broad Issues Concerning Judgment and Decision Bias

Hirshleifer provides a set of organizing principles to place the above phenomena into a systematic structure. He argues that three principles provide a unified explanation for most biases. First, people rely on heuristics because people face cognitive limitations. Because of a shared evolutionary history, people might be predisposed to rely on the same heuristics, and therefore be subject to the same biases. In this regard, he mentions work on fast and frugal heuristics, as described in Todd and Gigerenzer (2000). Second, the work of Trivers (1985, 1991) suggests that people inadvertently signal their inner states to others. For this reason, nature might have selected for traits such as overconfidence, in order that people signal strong confidence to others. This occurs because people who are well calibrated find it impossible to signal strong confidence credibly. Third, people's judgments and decisions are subject to their own emotions as well as to their reason.

Heuristic Simplification

Hirshleifer divides the items associated with heuristic simplification into several subcategories. The first category relates to attention, memory, and processing. Items include salience and availability effects such as underweighting the probability of events not explicitly available for consideration, the use of habits as a way of economizing on thinking, misattribution stemming from halo effects, misjudgments about truth stemming from ease of processing, cue competition, and familiarity bias. In this last respect, Trivers (1985) suggests that for evolutionary reasons, people prefer familiar and similar individuals for reasons having to do with genetic relatedness. Hirshleifer provides financial examples for some of these items, such as the halo effect explaining why growth stocks tend to be overpriced, and familiarity explaining why investors appear to exhibit a preference for local stocks.

The second subcategory for heuristic simplification pertains to narrow framing, mental accounting, and reference effects. Biases associated with this subcategory largely relate to oversimplification of a decision task, perhaps because time and cognitive resources are limited. Prospect theory, which is discussed in detail below, lies at the center of this subcategory, with its focus on framing effects especially the isolation effect, loss aversion, and reference points. The subcategory also includes a variety of effects motivated by or associated with prospect theory, such as the house money effect, regret, preference reversal, the endowment effect, status quo bias, and anchoring. Hirshleifer cites a few financial applications such as the disposition effect in connection with mental accounting and money illusion in connection with framing.

The third category relates to representativeness, the tendency to overrely on how representative an object is of the population from which it is drawn. In some situations, representativeness can lead people to underestimate unconditional population frequencies, a phenomenon known as "base rate underweighting." Representativeness can lead people to overweight recent evidence (recency bias), draw inferences which are too strong in the face of small samples ("law of small numbers"), overpredict reversals when they know the process governing transitions ("gambler's fallacy"), and overpredict continuation when they infer the process from recent observations ("hot hand fallacy"). As an application, Hirshleifer cites the experimental work of Andreassen and Kraus (1990), who found that in the presence of modest stock price fluctuations, subjects exhibit gambler's fallacy, but in the presence of a strong trend exhibit hot hand fallacy.

The fourth and final subcategory relates to subtleties in the updating of beliefs. In some types of situations people tend to predict reversals, whereas in others they predict continuation. Similarly, representativeness suggests that people underweight base rate information, whereas Edwards (1968) finds evidence that in some types of situations, people underweight singular information relative to base rate information. The challenge is to identify the relevant situations which give rise to each. Part of the explanation might involve cognitive processing costs and salience. This is why people might be predisposed to underweight information that is abstract and statistical such as probabilistic information and sample size, but overreact to scenarios and concrete examples which are more easily processed. Griffin and Tversky (1992) present a framework to address this issue, based on the distinction between the "strength" of evidence (such as how extreme or salient is the information) and the "weight" of evidence (such as how statistically relevant is the information to prediction).

Self-deception

Overconfidence is a form of self-deception, along with cognitive dissonance, biased self-attribution, hindsight bias, and confirmatory bias. In all of these cases, people feel better about themselves than they might were they bias-free. Overconfident people take pride in feeling that they have more ability than is actually the case and that they know more than is actually the case. Cognitive dissonance leads people to feel better about choices they made, even if the choices were nonoptimal. Biased self-attribution leads people to feel that their skills were responsible for their successes, and that external factors were responsible for their failures. Hindsight bias leads people to feel that their forecasting skills are better than is actually the case. Confirmatory bias leads people to feel better about their views because they underweight evidence that disconfirms their views, but overweight evidence that supports their views. At the same time, Klayman and Ha (1987) suggest that confirmatory bias might be an efficient mental shortcut rather than the result of self-deception.

Emotions and Self-control

The emotion of fear exerts an important influence on the way people make choices about risky alternatives. Many fear choices that are ambiguous about the risk involved, possibly because they worry about hostile manipulation of the odds they face.

Mood also appears to be an important determinant of how people feel about taking risk. Arkes et al. (1988) found that lottery ticket sales in Ohio increased after an Ohio State University football victory, presumably because the win elevated the moods of Ohio residents. Hirshleifer points out that mood exerts more of an impact on judgments about abstract issues than concrete issues for which people possess information.

Time Preference and Self-control

Neoclassical models tend to use exponential discounting, meaning a constant time-invariant discount factor to reflect impatience. There is a literature in psychology about hyperbolic discounting, where discount factors decrease more rapidly than is the case with exponential discounting. Hyperbolic discounting also gives rise to potential self-control difficulties when it comes to immediate gratification and the delay of unpleasantness. Applications of self-control to financial issues include savings, liquidity premia, and the equity premium puzzle.

2.1.2 Social Interactions

By and large the literature in behavioral finance draws from the psychology of individual behavior rather than social psychology. However, there have been some applications of social psychology to issues involving both investments and corporate finance. A key issue for investments concerns the process by which investors acquire information. In this respect, Shiller and Pound (1989) report that interpersonal communication drew investors' attention to the stocks they most recently had purchased. Shiller (1999) emphasizes the role of culture in communication, stressing that because of limited attention, investors attach special importance to ideas or facts which are reinforced by conversation or ritual. Kuran and Sunstein (1999) suggest that such interactions can produce "availability cascades" whereby topics under discussion publicly generate momentum, thereby reinforcing prior discussion.

A key bias studied in social psychology is the "conformity effect," the tendency of people's judgments and decisions to be skewed toward supporting other members of one's group. An example is Asch (1956) who found that people will report judgments that conform to the judgments of others in their group, even when they believe others to be in error. Stasser et al. (1989) report that people tend to discuss issues about which they have shared information rather than sharing which they hold privately. Stasser and Titus (1985) present evidence that people will withhold private information to avoid contradicting the views of others in their group.

The literature in social psychology has identified other biases. For example, because people tend to emphasize main points in conversation and deemphasize qualifying details, listeners tend to form beliefs that are too extreme Allport and Postman (1947), Anderson (1932). Another example is "fundamental attribution error" where people, in the course of determining the behavior of others, overestimate the importance of disposition and underestimate the role of external circumstances. Finally, in the "false consensus effect," people come to believe that others share their beliefs to a greater degree than is actually the case: see Ross et al. (1977). Hirshleifer describes several applications of these biases. For example, Welch (2000) describes the results of a survey of financial economists in connection with the equity premium, and reports a false consensus effect in this regard.

2.1.3 Modeling Alternatives to Expected Utility

Allais (1953) presented a set of paradoxes demonstrating that people are unlikely to behave in accordance with expected utility theory. Camerer (1995) describes a series of alternative frameworks, of which the most prominent is prospect theory, (Kahneman and Tversky, 1979).

In prospect theory, the carriers of value (meaning arguments of the utility function) are gains and losses relative to a pre-specified reference point. The value function is S-shaped so that it is concave in the domain of gains and convex in the domain of losses. The value function also features a kink at the origin, where it is steeper for losses than gains. Probabilities are distorted by a probability weighting function in which extremely low probabilities are treated as zero, moderately low probabilities are overweighted, and moderately high probabilities are underweighted.

2.1.4 Broad Asset Pricing Issues

Hirshleifer's survey focuses on the impact of investor psychology on asset pricing, relating to what he calls "the heart of the grand debate in finance spanning the last two decades." He begins his discussion with two presentations of asset pricing, Campbell (2000) and Cochrane (2000) who emphasize how expected returns are related to "objective external sources of risk." Hirshleifer suggests that what differentiates the behavioral approach from the neoclassical approach is its focus on how expected returns are related to both risk and to investor misvaluation. In this regard, he describes a conceptual starting point, a linear framework like the CAPM in which expected return is a function of two variables, one associated with objective risk and the other with a proxy for mispricing.

Hirshleifer makes an interesting point about the impact of irrational investors on asset prices, namely that in equilibrium arbitrage is a double-edged sword. Whereas rational investors move prices closer to their efficient levels, irrational investors move prices away from efficient levels. He asserts that in consequence, equilibrium prices reflect a weighted average of the different investors' beliefs. As a result, rational investors need not eliminate mispricing through their trades.

Consider where mispricing is most likely to be severe. One possibility is where information is sparse and arrives slowly, what Hirshleifer describes as "the dusty, idiosyncratic corners of the market." However, because of cognitive limitations, there might not be any perfectly rational investors in the market. As a result, systematic factors as well as idiosyncratic factors might be persistently mispriced. Moreover, the magnitude of mispricing might depend on the degree to which investors not subject to bias might have detected a profitable opportunity and are seeking to exploit it. Rational investors might have difficulty in knowing the degree to which other like minded investors are attempting to exploit the same profit opportunity.

The neoclassical view is that wealth flows from foolish to smart investors, so that in the long-run prices are set by rational investors. The behavioral view, developed in a series of papers by DeLong et al. (1990a,b, 1991) is that if foolish investors underestimate risk and take on more than would be rational, the additional premium earned might counter the flow of wealth to rational investors. The same argument might serve to explain how irrational investors induce persistent cross-section return predictability over the long-term. Again, the wealth flow to rational investors which stem from the mistakes of irrational investors is countered by the irrational investors earning a higher risk premium from their exposure to aggregate market risk.

Hirshleifer describes challenges respectively faced by those in the neoclassical school and those in the behavioral school. The neoclassical challenge is to identify objective risks to explain the various puzzles and anomalies. The behavioral challenge is identify how irrational investors can persistently affect prices when they are losing wealth to rational investors.

2.2 Barberis and Thaler (2003): Review of Behavioral Asset Pricing Literature

Barberis and Thaler (2003) suggest that behavioral finance has two main building blocks, namely psychology and the limits to arbitrage. By psychology they mean systematic departures from rationality of beliefs (Bayes' rule) and rationality of preferences (expected utility maximization). Departures from Bayes' rule occur because of heuristics and biases described in Hirsheleifer's survey. In the behavioral models discussed by Barberis and Thaler, expected utility maximization is replaced by prospect theory. Barberis and Thaler also discuss a phenomenon known as ambiguity aversion, which applies to the case of uncertainty. Limits to arbitrage refer to obstacles preventing arbitrage by fully rational agents from eliminating price inefficiencies.

2.2.1 Aggregate Stock Market

One of the most important applications of behavioral ideas to explaining aggregate stock market movements involves a triplet of puzzles involving the equity premium, risk-free rate, market volatility, and predictability of returns. The source of these puzzles is the inability of a standard neoclassical representative investor model, with plausible parameters, to explain the magnitude of the historical equity premium, return volatility, and return predictability in the U.S. market. The neoclassical model implies an equity premium of 0.1 percent, not the historical 3.9 percent. It implies a return standard deviation of 12 percent, not the historical 18 percent. And it implies an absence of predictability, in contrast to evidence of predictability.

The main behavioral approach to explaining the equity premium involves the work of Benartzi and Thaler (1995) and Barberis et al. (2001a). Both approaches use a representative investor whose preferences are based on prospect theory. While neoclassical expected utility theory emphasizes risk aversion in respect to total consumption or wealth on the part of investors, prospect theory emphasizes loss aversion in respect to changes in consumption or wealth. Behavioral theories of the equity premium puzzle focus on how short investment time horizons might induce loss averse investors to behave as if they were extremely averse to risk, thereby inducing a high equity premium in the market. In addition, if investors are concerned they have ambiguous beliefs about stock market returns, then they might demand an ambiguity aversion premium, thereby putting upward pressure on the equity premium.

Behavioral explanations for the volatility puzzle are based on both beliefs and preferences. The starting point for the puzzle is the price–dividend ratio, based on the work of LeRoy and Porter (1981) and Shiller (1981). A quick way of introducing the main issue is through the well-known Gordon constant expected growth formula which can be stated as $\frac{P_t}{D_{t+1}} = \frac{1}{r-g}$, where P denotes price, D denotes dividend, r denotes required return, and g denotes the expected dividend growth rate. This formula indicates the price–dividend ratio is driven by required return and expected dividend growth. If these are stable over time, then the neoclassical theory predicts that the price–dividend ratio should also be stable.

In practice, the price–dividend ratio is quite volatile, thereby prompting the question of whether volatility in the dividend growth rate or required return is sufficient to explain the puzzle. Although there is little evidence to suggest that the long-run dividend growth rate is volatile, the required return on stocks is a function of the risk-free rate, degree of market risk, and overall risk aversion. Barberis and Thaler point out that it is difficult to reconcile the volatility of the price–dividend ratio in terms of volatile interest rates or volatile risk. As to volatile risk aversion, they mention the work of Campbell and Cochrane (1999) who develop a habit formation model in which investors become more risk averse as their consumption falls toward the level to which they have become habituated.

Barberis and Thaler argue that behavioral explanations based on representativeness suggest that investors' expectations about future dividend growth and risk display excessive volatility relative to recent events. For example, investors might view a recent spurt in dividend growth as "representative" of the long-run sustainable future growth rate, thereby leading subjective g to exceed objective g. A similar statement might apply to perceived risk.

A behavioral explanation of the volatility puzzle based on preferences is similar in spirit to the behavioral explanation for the equity premium puzzle. In contrast to neoclassical expected utility theory, in which investors are assumed to be risk averse and have stable attitudes toward risk, prospect theory emphasizes that attitude toward risk is nonconstant and varies according to whether outcomes are registered as gains or as losses. Barberis et al. (2001a) develop a model with a representative investor whose preferences reflect elements of prospect theory and hedonic editing (Thaler and Johnson, 1990). In their model, investors become more tolerant of a loss after a rise in the market has generated gains for investors, and more averse to a loss after a drop in the market reduces that gain. Moreover, in line with hedonic editing, if the drop in the market leads investors to experience losses relative to the amount they originally invested, then they will become much more averse to further loss.

2.2.2 Cross-section of Average Returns

Behavioral finance is most associated with the anomalies literature, whereby patterns associated with the cross-section of average stock returns cannot be explained in terms of the capital asset pricing model. Among the most notable anomalies that cannot be explained on a CAPM risk-adjusted basis are the following:

1. Size premium: stocks with low market capitalization have subsequently earned higher returns than stocks with high market capitalization.

2. Long-term reversals: losers based on prior 36 month performance have subsequently outperformed winners based on the same criterion, over 60 months.
3. Scaled price-ratios: stocks associated with high ratios for book-to-market (BM) and earnings-to-price (EP) have subsequently outperformed stocks associated with lower ratios during the next year.
4. Momentum: winners based on prior short-term month performance (less than one year) have subsequently outperformed losers based on the same criterion during the next year.
5. Post-earnings-announcement drift: stocks associated with positive earnings surprises have subsequently outperformed stocks associated with negative earnings surprises during the next year.
6. Dividend initiations and omissions: For a year after the announcement, stocks associated with dividend initiations have subsequently outperformed the market, whereas stocks associated with dividend omissions have subsequently underperformed the market.
7. New Issues and Repurchases: Stocks of firms that have issued new (repurchased) equity have subsequently underperformed (outperformed) a control group of firms matched on size and book-to-market equity over a five (four) year period.

Fama and French (1993, 1996) develop a three-factor model which empirically captures many of the anomalies, and for which they provide a neoclassical risk-based interpretation. The factors relate to the market return, the difference in returns between small firms and large firms, and the difference in returns between high and low stocks ranked by BM.

Barberis and Thaler raise two concerns in connection with the Fama–French risk-based explanation. First, the return to low BM stocks tends to be below the risk-free rate. Second, neoclassical theory measures risk by the covariance of returns with the marginal utility of aggregate consumption growth. In this regard, the risk to a security is that it will pay a low return in bad times when the marginal utility of consumption growth is high. Therefore, a security earns a risk premium for generating a low return in bad times when aggregate consumption growth is low. However, there is little if any empirical support that stocks earning above average returns perform especially poorly during periods of low aggregate consumption growth.

There are a variety of behavioral belief-based models that have been developed to explain cross-sectional patterns. These models emphasize the combination of momentum in the short-term and reversals stemming from overreaction in the long-term.

Barberis et al. (1998) develop a model involving a risk neutral representative investor whose beliefs are biased by conservatism and representativeness. Their model features a risk-free security and a risky security. Conservatism leads the representative investor to underreact to new information unless the new information is part of a run, in which case representativeness leads the representative investor to overreact to the run. When overreaction leads the risky security to become mispriced, a subsequent correction eventually results.

Daniel et al. (1998, 2001) develop a model in which prices reflect the beliefs of a risk-neutral investor whose biases stem from overconfidence and self-attribution bias. In this behavioral combination, self-attribution bias leads the price-setting investor to be overconfident about information which he has generated on his own (his "private signal") relative to information which is publicly available. The model produces momentum when external events confirm the price-setting investor's private signal, thereby increasing the investor's overconfidence. However, when the excessive weight applied to the private signal leads the risky security to be mispriced, overreaction and a subsequent correction eventually result.

Hong and Stein (1999) present a model featuring the interaction between "newswatchers" who base their trades on privately observed fundamentals and "momentum traders" who base their trades on the most recent price change. Privately observed "news" diffuses slowly into prices, at which point momentum traders amplify the effect. The resulting momentum and subsequent positive feedback effect operate like a mechanical thermostat which does not click off when the correct temperature is reached. The resulting overreaction eventually leads to a correction. Hong and Stein do not emphasize particular psychological biases in their approach, although the traits of "newswatchers" are similar to those of the price-setting agents in the model developed by Daniel et al. Perhaps, momentum traders suffer from confirmation bias and the opposite of aversion to ambiguity, to the extent that they rely solely on technical analysis and fail to generate information about fundamentals.

Chopra et al. (1992) and La Porta et al. (1997) find that long-term reversals associated with past winners and losers as well (low BM stocks) appear to occur at the time of earnings are announced. Barberis and Thaler suggest that these findings reflect investors receiving news that their past forecasts, driven by representativeness, were extreme. Hong et al. (2000) find that momentum is more pronounced in the stocks of small cap firms and firms with low analyst coverage. They suggest that this finding supports a hypothesis stemming from the Hong–Stein model.

A series of papers discuss the implications associated with heterogeneous beliefs in combination with restrictions on short sales. See Miller (1977), Diether et al. (2004), Chen et al. (2002), and Jones and Lamont (2002). Short-sales restrictions create an asymmetry in which the beliefs of optimistic investors carry more weight in price formation than the beliefs of pessimistic investors. In this regard, the evidence indicates that increased breadth of ownership or higher costs of shorting will lead to upward bias in price and subsequent lower returns. Harrison and Kreps (1978) and Scheinkman and Xiong (2003) point out that in the presence of short-sale constraints, investors who believe a security is overvalued might choose to buy the security in anticipation of selling it later to investors who are especially optimistic. Hong and Stein (2003) suggest that pessimistic investors who cannot short an overvalued stock will buy the stock after its price declines to fundamental value, but not if its price increases. This leads to an asymmetric volatility response leading to skewness in the return distribution.

The model developed by Barberis and Huang (2001) explains the value premium associated with BM by suggesting that loss aversion and narrow framing lead investors to act as if they are more averse to risk after a stock has declined in price. The dynamics are similar to the model developed by Barberis et al. (2001a).

Although the behavioral models described above were developed to explain the cross-section of returns, it is worth noting that they all feature a single risky asset rather than multiple assets whose returns are jointly determined. This means that the explanations associated with these models, are at best suggestive of the role played by underlying psychological phenomena.

A similar statement holds in respect to explanations of the closed-end puzzle (Lee et al., 1991). The puzzle concerns the existence of a closed-end fund discount (or premium, when positive) relative to net asset value. The behavioral approach to the puzzle is based on the notion that investor sentiment varies over time, fluctuating between degrees of optimism and pessimism. Pessimistic sentiment produces closed-end fund discounts whereas optimistic sentiment produces closed-end fund premiums. The sentiment-based explanation suggests that closed-end fund prices will covary in response to changing sentiment. In equilibrium, rational investors will demand a positive risk premium as compensation for bearing the component of risk associated with changes in investor sentiment as well as the component associated with changing fundamentals.

One of the most important aspects of the behavioral approach to risk premiums is the idea that the premium can be decomposed into a fundamental component and a systematic sentiment component, where sentiment is understood to mean excessive optimism or pessimism. In this respect, being "systematic" means that sentiment should also explain the premiums associated with small cap stocks, high BM stocks, and so on. Barberis and Thaler point out that the discount attached to closed-end funds as a class and premium attached to small cap stocks covary. They also review work by Fama and French (1993, 1995) showing the existence of common factors in earnings and returns associated with small cap stocks. In this regard, they emphasize that while such common factors exist, they are weaker for earnings than for returns, thereby suggesting that other issues are at work. Barberis and Shleifer (2003) suggest that investors are prone to "categorization" and treat certain members of certain groups of stocks (such as small cap stocks) as being more similar than fundamentals warrant. As a result, categorization produces common factors in returns to stocks in the same group. A pertinent example of a group is the S&P 500. See Barberis et al. (2001b) who document the impact of a stock's beta when the stock is first included in the index.

2.2.3 Investor Behavior

Barberis and Thaler discuss how psychology influences the behavior of individual investors, an issue they describe as being less controversial than issues involving the determinants of market prices. They introduce the discussion by mentioning the trend toward increased participation in equities and the increased emphasis on defined contribution plans in retirement planning.

Individual investors do not choose mean-variance portfolios. Instead, their portfolios tend to be insufficiently diversified. Benartzi and Thaler (2001) suggest that ambiguity aversion and the desire for familiarity lead investors to exhibit "home bias," the tendency to overweight securities with which investors are familiar. French and Poterba (1991) document the high concentrations of domestic equity in the equity portion of investors' portfolios in the USA, Japan, and the United Kingdom Grinblatt and Keloharju (2001a) find that Finnish investors concentrate on the stocks of firms that are located close to them geographically. Huberman (2001) documents a regional bias in the holding of stocks of regional telephone companies. Benartzi (2001) reports a strong bias toward own company stock in 401(k) plans. Investors might also choose poorly diversified portfolios because they use crude heuristics, such as the "1/n" heuristic which involves dividing assets equally across choices. See Benartzi and Thaler (2001) who report evidence of instances in which the relative number of equity funds appears to drive the portion of participants' allocations toward equity.

Many investors trade excessively and unprofitably. Barber and Odean (2000) find that for individual investors, risk-adjusted portfolio returns are negatively correlated with the frequency of trading. They attribute this result to a combination of overconfidence and transaction costs. That is, overconfident investors mistakenly believe that their skills are sufficiently high to compensate for the costs of trading.

In terms of the selling decision, investors are prone to pay more tax than necessary because they sell winners too quickly and hold losers too long. Shefrin and Statman (1985) call this behavior "the disposition effect" and attribute it to the following series of psychological phenomena: the reference point property, mental accounting, regret aversion, and self-control. A key feature of the disposition effect for stocks is that the original purchase price serves as the reference point. Using discount brokerage data, Odean (1998a) provides strong evidence of the disposition effect. Genesove and Mayer (2001) present evidence from the housing market that homeowners are reluctant to sell their homes at prices below original purchase price. As study by Coval and Shumway (2005) demonstrates that the disposition effect is not confined to individual investors. Professional traders in the Treasury Bond futures pit at the Chicago Board of Trade take greater intraday risks in the afternoon if they have incurred losses in the morning. Barberis and Thaler do touch on issues of pricing in connection with the disposition effect. They describe work by Grinblatt and Han (2004) which indicates that the disposition effect might underlie momentum. Momentum results after gains when investors who are eager to take profits after good news retard the adjustment of price to fundamental value. Momentum results after losses when investors who are eager to hold their stocks after bad news retard the adjustment of price to fundamental value.

In terms of the buying decision, Odean (1999) and Barber and Odean (2008) find that investors are prone to buy stocks to which their attention has recently been drawn. Operationally, attention for stocks is based on one or more of the following traits: abnormally high trading volume, extreme returns, and stocks with news announcements.

2.3 Baker et al. (2007): Survey of Corporate Finance

Baker et al. (2007b) provide a two-pronged approach in surveying the literature on behavioral corporate finance. The first prong pertains to the impact of irrational investor behavior on rational corporate managers, while the second prong pertains to the manner in which irrational decisions by corporate managers impact corporate value.

2.3.1 The Irrational Investors Approach

There are several reasons to believe that some corporate managers might have the ability to identify mispricing. First, they have superior information about their own firms. In this respect there is evidence that corporate managers earn abnormal returns on their own trades. See Muelbroek (1992), Seyhun (1992), and Jenter (2005). Second, they are less constrained by the limits of arbitrage than equally smart money managers. Third, managers might have access to efficient heuristics: see Baker and Stein (2004).

Consider how rational managers might function in a world in which irrational investors cause inefficiencies in market prices. Baker et al. suggest that these managers balance three objectives: (1) maximizing fundamental value; (2) undertaking actions to boost the market value of their firms above fundamental value (catering); and (3) undertaking financing decisions to exploit temporary mispricings of the securities issued by their firms (market timing).

Theory

Baker et al. develop a model to capture the criterion function a rational manager uses to balance these objectives. For this purpose, think about a neoclassical firm whose investment and financing strategies are determined independently. Define e as the deviation in the firm's book value of equity from its optimal neoclassical level. Let K be the amount of capital invested, $f(K,e)$ be a function specifying the present value of future cash flows inclusive of financing effects, and λ be a number between 0 and 1 measuring the degree to which the manager's horizon is long-term. The product $e\delta$ represents the value transfer to original shareholders from exploiting the mispricing. The criterion function has the form:

$$\lambda[f(K;) - K + e\delta(\cdot)] + (1 - \lambda)\delta(\cdot). \tag{2.1}$$

The first-order conditions for this problem are as follows:

$$f_K = 1 - \left(e + \frac{(1-\lambda)}{\lambda}\right)\delta_K, \tag{2.2}$$

$$-f_e = \delta(\cdot) + \left(e + \frac{(1-\lambda)}{\lambda}\right)\delta_e. \tag{2.3}$$

In the neoclassical benchmark for Equation (2.1) managers have a long-term horizon ($\lambda = 1$) and there is no mispricing ($\delta = 0$). In this case, Equation (2.2) states that $f_K = 1$ (meaning the net present value of investment is zero at the margin) and $e = f_e(0) = 0$.

Consider how choices of K and e are impacted by $\lambda < 1$ and $\delta \neq 0$. Begin with Equation (2.2). Suppose that $\delta_K > 0$, meaning higher K exacerbates overpricing. In this case, Equation (2.2) implies that $f_K < 1$, so that managers cater to investor sentiment by increasing K relative to the neoclassical case.

Next consider Equation (2.3). Consider the case in which $\delta > 0$ (overpricing) combined with $\delta_e < 0$. The inequality means that when the firm issues more equity, the resulting selling pressure leads the degree of overpricing to decline. In this case, Equation (2.3) is analogous to the microeconomic problem faced by a monopolist who chooses quantity to equate marginal revenue and marginal cost. In this analogy, e corresponds to quantity and δ corresponds to price. The right-hand side of Equation (2.3) corresponds to the two terms making up marginal revenue, while the left-hand side corresponds to marginal cost. In this respect, when $e > 0$, the firm takes on too much equity relative to debt, thereby losing tax shield and related benefits, in which case $f_e < 0$. Equation (2.3) indicates that the firm chooses $e > 0$, up to the point in the monopoly analogy whereby marginal revenue equals marginal cost.

There is also the case $\delta < 0$ (underpricing). A firm that is financially constrained would find itself unable or unwilling to raise external financing, so that e might be negative with $f_e > 0$. For managers with long enough horizons (λ sufficiently close to 1), Equation (2.2) would imply low investment as $f_K > 1$. Such firms are reluctant to issue underpriced equity in order to finance investment.

Empirical Studies Involving Real Investment

Most research about real investment and mispricing focuses on the case of overpricing. Baker et al. review some of the early literature on this topic, beginning with Keynes' discussion about "animal spirits" during the 1920s, and moving on to other bubble episodes involving electronics (1959–1962), growth stocks (1967–1968), and dot-com stocks (late 1990s). They point out that the first modern empirical studies were inconclusive about the impact of mispricing on the magnitude of investment. These studies sought to control for fundamental value and searched for a residual effect on investment from stock prices.

The authors of later studies searched for evidence that proxies for mispricing impact investment. Chirinko and Schaller (2001, 2004), Panageas (2003), Polk and Sapienza (2004), and Gilchrist et al. (2004) find such evidence. Polk and Sapienza also show that this impact is greater for shorter managerial horizons, as happens when share turnover is higher. Following Stein (1996), Baker et al. (2003) study whether investment will be most sensitive to mispricing for equity-dependent firms, the case discussed above where $e < 0$.

Baker et al. point out that open questions remain about the magnitude of the mispricing-investment effect and the associated efficiency implications. In this last respect, Polk and Sapienza (2004) find that in the cross-section, firms that invest more earn lower subsequent returns. Titman et al. (2004) find the same pattern, and Lamont (2000) reports something similar in a time series analysis. Nevertheless, Baker et al. do not view these results as strong evidence of inefficiency in an ex ante sense, and claim not to be convinced that the pattern stems from catering.

Managers might use mergers and acquisitions to cater to investor sentiment, perhaps by using the overvalued stock of their own firms to acquire less overvalued targets, or by engaging in a combination for which sentiment is positive, see Shleifer and Vishny (2003). This theory offers some insight into the time-series relationship between merger volume and stock prices. It also explains why cash acquirers subsequently outperform stock acquirers (who earn negative long-run returns), see Loughran and Vijh (1997) and Rau and Vermaelen (1998).

Evidence of a positive correlation between market-level mispricing and merger volume can be found in Dong et al. (2003), and Ang and Cheng (2009). These studies report that undervalued targets are more likely to be hostile to acquisition, and that overpriced acquirers tend to pay higher takeover premiums. Moreover, subsequent returns to mergers conducted during high-valuation periods tend to be poor (Bouwman et al., 2009).

Baker et al. pose an interesting question about mispricing-driven mergers: why would an overvalued firm use a merger instead of issuing more equity? They suggest a framing-based explanation that a merger might be more effective at hiding the underlying misvaluation. Baker et al. (2004) also propose that investors might respond more passively to accepting the acquirer's shares as part of the merger (a form of status quo bias), but would not actively purchase those shares when issued directly.

An issue related to mergers and acquisition is the diversification discount. Although there is little in the behavioral finance literature dealing with this issue, Baker et al. suggest that the 1960's conglomerate wave reflected a desire by managers to cater to investors' preference for conglomerates. They discuss the work of Klein (2001) who finds a diversification premium of 36 percent in the period 1966–1968, followed by a decline between July 1968 and June 1970, as reported in Ravenscraft and Scherer (1987).

Empirical Studies Involving Financial Policy

As was mentioned in the theoretical section above, mispricing can lead a firm's managers to engage in market timing, for example by issuing new shares when equity is overpriced and by repurchasing shares when equity is underpriced. Survey evidence presented by Graham and Harvey (2001) indicates that financial managers view such market timing activities as very important. Jenter (2005) presents related evidence that managers conduct secondary equity offerings (SEOs) while simultaneously engaging in insider selling.

There is considerable empirical evidence suggesting market timing in respect to equity. Loughran et al. (1994) report a high positive correlation between volume of initial public offerings (IPOs) and international stock market valuations. As for seasoned equity offerings (SEOs), Marsh (1982) reports that equity issuance increases after recent stock market appreciation. Loughran and Ritter (1995) provide evidence suggesting the presence of mispricing. Relative to a size-matched firm, after five years the average IPO underperforms its non-IPO peer by 30 percent. After reviewing the relevant literature, Baker et al. conclude that on average U.S. firms issuing equity subsequently underperform the market by between 20 and 40 percent over five years. At the same time, they also point out that the equity market timing issue is controversial, and is still a subject of considerable debate.

In terms of share repurchases, Brav et al. (2005) report survey evidence indicating that the great majority of firms agree that they repurchase shares when they view their shares as underpriced in the market. Indeed, Ikenberry et al. (1995) find that the average repurchaser outperformed firms matched by size and book-to-market equity by 12 percent over the subsequent four years. See also Ikenberry et al. (2000). Dichev (2004) reports that firms who engaged in market timing reduced their cost of capital by 1.3 percent a year.

Moving from equity to debt, the survey evidence presented by Graham and Harvey (2001) does indicate that firms issue debt when they feel that interest rates are low. Moreover, firms tend to issue short-term debt when the yield curve is steep, and when waiting for long-term rates to fall. Marsh (1982) reports that in his sample of U.K. firms, interest rates impacted the debt–equity choice. Using a sample of U.S. firms, Guedes and Opler (1996) report that firms do indeed issue short maturity debt when the yield curve is steeply sloped, and longer maturity debt when the yield curve is flatter or negatively sloped. In this respect, empirically subsequent bond returns are positively correlated with the slope of the yield curve, thereby supporting the market timing decisions managers make about debt issuance. Moreover, the Graham–Harvey survey evidence indicates that 44 percent of firms engage in cross-border market timing to exploit differential interest rates. In this respect, Froot and Dabora (1999) present evidence of cross-border mispricing, while Henderson et al. (2009) report that subsequent to periods of high foreign issues, returns tend to be low.

Interestingly, Richardson and Sloan (2003) find that equity returns tend to be low after debt issuance, suggesting that firms might be timing their idiosyncratic credit quality. That said, there are other explanations for the pattern. For example, as equity valuation is a component of the cost of debt, equity overvaluation might make debt cheap. Therefore, firms issue debt because it is cheap, and the overvalued equity subsequently corrects itself.

If managers engage in market timing, and are also subject to status quo bias, then firms which issue equity when they believe their stocks are overpriced will tend to feature low leverage. Baker and Wurgler (2002) provide such a market timing-based explanation of capital structure. Their analysis employs a weighted measure of market-to-book equity, where the weights are based on the degree of external financing. A high value of this ratio suggests that the firm raised the bulk of its external equity or debt when its market-to-book ratio was high. According to the theory, in the cross-section the weighted average will be negatively related to debt-to-assets. Despite the evidence supporting the prediction, Baker et al. point out that the issue is still under debate. One issue is that the relationship Baker and Wurgler identify might stem from growth opportunities rather than market timing. See Hovakimian (2006).

Other Corporate Decisions

Besides investment and financial policy, behavioral phenomena play a role in other corporate decisions such as dividends, choice of firm name, earnings management, and executive compensation.

The major issue in respect to dividends is whether firms cater to investor sentiment by initiating dividends when sentiment is positive and omitting dividends when sentiment is negative. Baker et al. (2003) measure a "dividend premium" as the difference between average market-to-book equity between payers and nonpayers. They claim to find evidence of catering by noting that initiations increase when the dividend premium is high, and omissions increase when the dividend premium is negative. Baker and Wurgler (2004a,b) suggest that catering might explain the result described in Fama and French (2001) about the sharp decline between 1978 and 1999 of the number of firms that pay dividends. However, they also note that the catering theory of dividends is limited in that it only explains initiations and omissions, not the magnitude of dividends. In addition, catering as defined above, does not address other psychological issues associated with dividends such as self-control, regret aversion, and hedonic editing (Shefrin and Statman, 1984).

Cooper et al. (2001) presented evidence that during the Internet bubble, many small firms changed their name to include a "dotcom" reference. They noted that consistent with a catering motive, such name changes resulted in an average announcement effect of 74 percent.

A survey conducted by Graham et al. (2004) found that financial managers believe that investors care more about earnings per share (EPS) than cash flows, and for this reason are willing to sacrifice net present value for higher EPS. For this reason, earnings manipulation is a form of catering. Teoh et al. (1998a,b) report that firms who most aggressively manage earnings are associated with the highest underperformance in connection with equity issuance. Bergstresser et al. (2004) found that as CEO compensation becomes more sensitive to share price, earnings management increases. Sloan (1996) finds that firms associated with high accruals tend to feature low subsequent returns.

2.3.2 The Irrational Managers Approach

Consider the opposite side of the coin, where market prices are efficient, but corporate managers are subject to psychological pitfalls. The most common pitfalls in the behavioral corporate finance literature are unrealistic optimism and overconfidence. Here unrealistic optimism is typically interpreted as overestimating the first moment of cash flows or returns, and overconfidence is interpreted as underestimating the second moment (risk as measured by the standard deviation).

2.3.2.1 Theory

The theoretical framework for the case of irrational managers operating within efficient markets is similar in structure to the model used to study the case of rational managers operating within irrational markets.

A new variable γ is added to the model to represent the combination of managerial excessive optimism and overconfidence. An unbiased manager is associated with $\gamma = 0$. The criterion function has the form:

$$(1+\gamma)f(K;) - K - e\gamma f(K;). \tag{2.4}$$

The first-order conditions for this problem are as follows:

$$f_K = \frac{1}{1+(1-e)\gamma}, \tag{2.5}$$

$$(1+\gamma)f_e = \gamma(f(K;) + ef_e(K;)). \tag{2.6}$$

In the neoclassical benchmark for Equation (2.4) $\gamma = 0$. This results in the usual first-order conditions $f_K = 1$ and $f_e = 0$. When $\gamma > 0$ managers overinvest, and balance a shift away from the neoclassical capital structure against perceived losses from market timing. Suppose that $e > 0$. This happens when the firm is cash poor and chooses to issue more equity than is associated with the neoclassical case. Equation (6.1) implies that the degree of overinvestment falls, thereby leading to cash flow sensitivity. If there is an upper bound on leverage ($f_e > 0$), then a financial pecking order results, as managers never sell equity they perceive to be underpriced unless it is absolutely necessary in order to fund investment.

A collection of papers in the behavioral literature points out that unrealistic optimism and overconfidence can produce benefits in the presence of agency-related managerial traits that lead to underinvestment, such as risk aversion or debt overhang. (Gervais et al., 2003; Goel and Thakor, 2008; Hackbarth, 2009).

2.3.2.2 Empirical Issues

A key empirical task associated with the rational managers/inefficient market approach involves identifying proxies for mispricing. Baker et al. discuss a variety of possible measures, such as market-to-book as an ex ante measure and abnormal subsequent realized returns as an ex post measure.

By the same token, a key empirical task associated with the irrational managers/efficient market approach involves identifying proxies for excessive optimism and overconfidence. This is especially important in that the behavioral structure represented by Equation (2.4) is formally similar to an agency structure, with γ representing private managerial benefits and $e\gamma f(K;)$ being replaced by a function $c(e)$ corresponding to the agency cost of raising external equity. This means that overinvestment, underinvestment, cash flow sensitivity, and pecking order financing have both agency cost explanations and behavioral explanations. For this reason, identifying proxies which distinguish between the two possibilities is a critical task.

Malmendier and Tate (2005) suggest a longholder proxy for excessive optimism and overconfidence. The longholder proxy identifies chief executive officers (CEOs) by their propensity to hold in-the-money executive options on their own firm's stock until expiration. The point of the proxy is that because CEOs portfolios are overly concentrated in the value of their own firms, rational CEOs would exercise in-the-money options long before expiration, whereas excessively optimistic, overconfident CEOs would wait the expiration year to exercise. Malmendier and Tate find that cash flow sensitivity is pronounced among firms whose CEOs are longholders, and especially high when the firm is equity dependent.

There is ample evidence suggesting that excessive optimism and overconfidence lead to overinvestment. Merrow et al. (1981) and Statman and Tyebjee (1985) present evidence of excessive optimism in project cost forecasts. Cooper et al. (1988) report that 68 percent of entrepreneurs believe that their own startups are more likely to succeed than comparable firms. Moreover, only 5 percent believe the odds to be worse, and one-third perceive the risk of failure to be close to zero. Indeed, half of startups do not survive more than three years (Scarpetta et al., 2002). Given the undiversified nature of entrepreneurial investment, Moskowitz and Vissing-Jorgensen (2002) suggest that returns to private equity seem too low, a point to which I return in Section 6.

Landier and Thesmar (2009) survey French entrepreneurs. They find that 56 percent initially estimate that there will be "development" in the near future and only 6 percent expect difficulties. However, three years into their ventures, only 38 percent expect development and 17 percent expect difficulties. To counter excessive optimism and overconfidence, Landier and Thesmar discuss contracts which transfer control from entrepreneurs to investors when the former persist in following their initial plans, despite signals suggesting changes. They also suggest that because excessively optimistic, overconfident entrepreneurs underestimate short-term risks, they choose short-term financing over long-term financing, thereby losing control of their enterprises to investors more frequently than they planned.

Malmendier and Tate (2008) apply their longholder analysis to mergers and acquisitions. Roll (1986) suggested that hubris leads managers of acquiring firms to overpay for targets, thereby suffering from "the winner's curse." As it happens, longholder CEOs complete more mergers than longholders, especially diversifying mergers. In addition, longholder CEOs of the least equity dependent firms are more apt to engage in acquisitions, perhaps because they are least concerned about financing the acquisition with equity they believe to be underpriced.

Baker et al. also discuss behavioral managerial patterns distinct from excessive optimism and overconfidence. For example, the Graham–Harvey survey evidence indicates that many financial managers rely on heuristics such as the payback rule and use firm-wide discount rates to compute hurdle rates instead of risk-specific hurdle rates. More than half of firms use target debt–equity ratios, less than 10 percent set strict targets, and target debt–equity ratios tend to be based on book values instead of market values as called for in the neoclassical framework.

Managers also exhibit reference point effects. They are prone to "throw good money after bad:" (Statman and Sepe, 1989; Guedj and Scharfstein, 2004). Loughran and Ritter (2002) apply a portion of the framework presented by Shefrin and Statman (1984) to suggest that initial underpricing for IPOs is pronounced when the offer price lies above the upper end of the file range, thereby generating a perceived gain relative to the file range reference point. The argument is that this gain makes owner/managers more willing to accept underpricing.

2.4 Subrahmanyam (2007): Additional Perspectives

Subrahmanyam (2007) begins by identifying what he calls the central paradigms of modern finance, "all derived from investor rationality."

The paradigms are: (i) portfolio allocation based on expected return and risk, (ii) risk-based asset pricing models such as the CAPM and other similar frameworks, (iii) the Miller–Modigliani theorem and its augmentation by the theory of agency, and (iv) the pricing of contingent claims. His survey then focuses on how behavioral ideas have impacted these paradigms. To minimize discussion which overlaps the preceding three surveys, attention will focus on works that appeared subsequent to the earlier surveys, or ideas not covered.

2.4.1 Cross-Section of Stock Returns

The debate about whether risk or psychology explains the cross-section continues. Part of this debate focuses on the Fama and French (1993) three-factor model and a critique by Daniel and Titman (1997) centered on whether it is firm characteristics or factor loadings that explain returns. More recently, the debate has become more nuanced, focusing on whether factors proxy for both fundamentally based risk and sentiment. In this respect, Daniel and Titman (2006) suggest that the book-to-market effect is driven by overreaction to that part of the book-to-market ratio not related to accounting fundamentals. Moreover, they argue that the component of this ratio which relates to fundamentals does not actually forecast returns, bringing into question the "distress-risk" explanation.

Behavioral analyses of the cross-section focus on momentum in the short-run followed by reversals in the long-run. Hong et al. (2007) explain momentum, asset bubbles, and other phenomena using a model in which investors use overly simplified models to evaluate stocks. This type of model provides insight into the implications of investors relying on heuristics rather than full optimizing models. Kausar and Taffler (2006) provide evidence which supports the approach advanced by Daniel et al. (1998). They report that stocks initially exhibit momentum in response to an announcement that the firm is in distress (a going-concern audit report), but later exhibit reversals. Doukas and Petmezas (2005) find support for the self-attribution hypothesis, one of the elements of the Daniel et al.'s approach. However, they find the phenomenon in the market for corporate control, where managers appear to earn successfully smaller returns in each successive acquisition because they become increasingly overconfident with each successful acquisition. At the same time, there is mixed evidence about the regime switching hypotheses advanced by Barberis et al. (1998). Chan et al. (2003) find no support suggesting extrapolation after a sequence of news events within returns data. However, Frieder (2004) does find supporting evidence in order flow data around earnings announcements. Doukas and McKnight (2005) find that the results reported by Hong et al. (2000) hold in Europe, thereby providing out-of-sample confirmation for the Hong and Stein (1999) hypotheses.

Subrahmanyam points out that it is difficult for the neoclassical approach to justify the magnitude of Sharpe ratios observed in practice. Based on the Euler equation from a neoclassical representative investor model, a high Sharpe ratio implies highly variable marginal utility across states, for which there is little if any empirical support. (Hansen and Jagannathan, 1991). For theory to support a positive premium in respect to size and book-to-market equity, the returns of small and high book-to-market stocks would need to covary negatively with marginal utility. Given that marginal utility is inversely related to consumption growth, this implies that the returns associated with small cap firms and stocks with high book-to-market equity would need to be particularly high in good times, and vice versa. However, Lakonishok et al. (1994) find no evidence that this is the case. In a related vein, Haugen and Baker (1996) find that the strongest determinants of expected returns are past returns, trading volume and accounting ratios such as return on equity and price/earnings. Notably, they find no evidence that risk measures such as systematic or total volatility are material for the cross-section of equity returns.

The Barberis–Thaler survey discusses belief-based models with institutional friction. Subrahmanyam's treatment of this issue mentions the work of Baker and Stein (2004). Baker and Stein argue that optimistic investors generate volume, producing a negative relation between returns and past volume. Notably, the optimism is reversed in subsequent periods. However, because of short-selling constraints, pessimism is not adequately reflected in stock prices.

In cross-sectional regressions, stocks of small firms which have low analyst following appear to feature greater mispricing in terms of return predictability from book-to-market and momentum. (Zhang, 2006). There is evidence that mispricing is most severe for stocks where institutional ownership is lowest (Nagel, 2005) who suggests that institutional ownership is a proxy for short-selling constraints, in that short-selling is typically cheaper for institutions.

Some findings appear to lack mutual consistency. Subrahmanyam mentions a finding by Hvidkjaer (2006) whereby on net, small investors buy loser momentum stocks and subsequently become net sellers in these stocks. This suggests that they may create momentum by underreacting to negative information. Yet, Hvidkjaer (2005) reports a negative relationship between trade imbalances of small investors and future stock returns in the cross-section. This result is consistent with an overreaction effect by small investors, followed by the reversal of their sentiment, thereby generating stock return predictability.

Subrahmanyam discusses several papers concerning one of the central claims made in the behavioral finance literature, namely that investors who are imperfectly irrational are able to persist in the long run. The specific papers he mentions in this regard are DeLong et al. (1991), which is the seminal work mentioned earlier on this point, Kyle and Wang (1997), and Hirshleifer et al. (2006).

2.4.2 Other Psychological Influences on Returns

As was mentioned in Hirshleifer's survey, Griffin and Tversky (1992) provide a psychological theory based on weight and strength explaining why some situations feature underweighting of base rates, whereas other situations feature overweighting of base rates. Sorescu and Subrahmanyam (2006) test the argument that investors overreact to the strength of a signal and underreact to its weight. They proxy weight by analyst experience and strength by the number of categories spanned by analyst revisions. Doing so, they find some support for the Griffin and Tversky hypothesis.

Hirshleifer's survey mentions the role of emotions, especially mood, on returns. For example, consider the possibility that mood is positively correlated with exposure to sunlight. A study by Saunders (1993) documents that stock returns on the New York Stock Exchange tend to be positive on sunny days but mediocre on cloudy days. Extending this study to a number of international markets, Hirshleifer and Shumway (2003) confirm this finding. At the same time, Goetzmann and Zhu (2005) find little evidence that the return pattern stems from individual investors' trading patterns.

A related approach focuses on seasonal affective disorder (SAD). Kamstra et al. (2000) focus on returns for weekends involving the switch from daylight savings time to standard time. They find these returns to be very negative, and suggest that the cause is induced depression of investors subject to SAD. In a different type of mood study, Edmans et al. (2007) study how stock market returns in a country are impacted by the outcomes of sporting events involving that country. They find that returns are positive when the outcome is positive and vice versa. Although Subrahmanyam does not mention it explicitly, mood has also become a specific object of study in the neurofinance literature: see Knutson and Kuhnen (2009).

In discussing the disposition effect, Subrahmanyam describes a comprehensive study of trading activity by Grinblatt and Keloharju (2001b). They confirm the disposition effect in Finnish data. Finnish data is exceptionally rich, in that it is comprehensive on an account and trade-by-trade basis. Kaustia (2004) also provides insight into the disposition effect by focusing on IPO markets. The idea is that because the offer price is a common purchase price, the disposition effect will be clearly identifiable. Kaustia finds that volume is lower when the stock price is below the offer price. He also finds that there is a sharp upsurge in volume after the price rises above the offer price for the first time.

As to diversification, Goetzmann and Kumar (2008) find that the portfolios held by individual investors who are young and less wealthy are less diversified than older, more wealthy investors. In support of the familiarity hypothesis, Frieder and Subrahmanyam (2005) present evidence that individual investors prefer stocks with high brand recognition.

Poteshman and Serbin (2003) present evidence that option investors do not optimally exercise options. For example, they exercise options when they should instead sell them. Both Stein (1989) and Poteshman (2001) report that options implied volatility appears to reflect short-term overreaction. Evidence presented by Bakshi et al. (2000) suggests that traders often cause movements in option prices to be inconsistent with comparative statics based on traditional rationality assumptions.

2.5 Critique: Weaknesses in the Behavioral Approach

Behavioral finance has both strengths and weaknesses. The prior surveys do a good job of articulating its strengths, but not as a good job in articulating its weaknesses. Indeed, only Baker et al. strive to present an approach which is balanced by focusing on weaknesses as well as strengths. This issue is important, in that some of the weaknesses in the behavioral approach are foundational in nature, and need to be addressed for the behavioralizing of finance to be successful. In this section, I provide a brief description of what I see as key weaknesses in the behavioral approach. Addressing these issues underlies much of the remainder of this monograph.

2.5.1 Preferences

We do not yet have a coherent, systematic behavioral approach to preferences. Discussions about preferences in the behavioral finance literature are overwhelmingly dominated by prospect theory. To be sure, prospect theory offers important insights, and captures a wide variety of behavioral patterns observed in experimental settings. However, there is a difference between describing the empirical patterns and modeling those patterns. The literature in behavioral finance has a tendency to treat the patterns and the theory as one and the same, when in fact they are not.

Unfortunately, for all its richness, prospect theory is incomplete and its formal structure possesses some serious flaws. It is incomplete in respect to framing. The shape of the functional form used to capture probability weighting is sensitive to the choice of parameter value. In particular the shape is at odds with the principles underlying the theory (Ingersoll, 2008). The convex portion of its value function gives rise to boundary solutions that are highly unrealistic (Shefrin, 2008a). This feature presents difficulties in respect to the character of equilibrium (De Giorgi et al., 2009).

In introducing the disposition effect, Shefrin and Statman (1985) begin with elements of prospect theory. In this regard, Statman and I suggest that original purchase price serves as a likely reference point, concavity of the value function in the domain of gains suggests a tendency to realize winners, and convexity of the value function in the domain of losses suggests a tendency to hold losers. However, we were quick to indicate that prospect theory cannot provide a complete explanation for the disposition effect. We proposed that a series of additional psychological phenomena underlies the behavior. These phenomena included a realization utility mental accounting component, regret, and self-control. Our discussion of self-control indicated that some people could learn to reduce, if not eliminate, the tendency to exhibit the disposition effect.

My sense is that finance academics have been very slow to pick up on the nuances in Shefrin and Statman (1985). Only recently have there been a wave of papers addressing the inability of prospect theory to explain the disposition effect (Hens and Vlcek, 2005; Barberis and Xiong, 2009; Kaustia, 2009). In addition, Feng and Seasholes (2005) present evidence that people can learn to reduce their vulnerability to the disposition effect, which is consistent with the self-control discussion in Shefrin and Statman (1985).

Applications of prospect theory in the behavioral finance literature have also been piecemeal. For example, Barberis et al. (2001a) emphasize hedonic editing, but use a piecewise linear value function that does not conform to the specification in Tversky and Kahneman (1992). They also use probabilities rather than weights, as called for by Tversky and Kahneman (1992). In contrast, Barberis and Huang (2008) uses nonlinear probability weighting.

2.5.2 Cross-Section

Most of the behavioral asset pricing models to explain cross-sectional patterns do not actually model the cross-section. Instead they rely on models that feature, but a single risky security, and focus on overreaction and underreaction.

Taken together, the contributions to this literature are something of a behavioral hodge podge. Barberis et al. (1998) develop a model in which a representative investor makes rational use of Bayes' rule, but relative to a flawed regime switching model. Daniel et al. (1998) develop a model based on time varying overconfidence and biased self-attribution. Hong and Stein (1999) develop a model based on differential heuristics. Underlying all these models are a variety of interesting stories. However, taken together they do not provide for a unified, coherent, systematic behavioral approach to asset pricing.

In addition, reverse engineering has characterized the behavioral approach to underreaction, in that behavioral models have been constructed to explain the observed patterns rather than predict them. An exception is DeBondt and Thaler (1985) which formulated its prediction of overreaction based on Kahneman and Tversky (1973). However, the findings about underreaction took behaviorists by surprise.

2.5.3 Long-Run Dynamics

There is reason to believe that a key behavioral contention is in error. This is the claim that in the presence of rational investors, irrational investors will survive in the long-term because they take on excessive risk. The most influential paper in this regard is DeLong et al. (1991), see Subrahmanyam (2007). As it happens, the results in the latter paper are inconsistent with the general literature on long-run survivability (Blume and Easley, 2008). This is problematic. Rigor matters.

2.5.4 Contingent Claims

The contingent claims approach has provided finance with a framework to unify a series of different models of asset pricing and portfolio choice. An excellent treatment of this approach is Cochrane (2005), who develops asset pricing theory around the concept of a stochastic discount factor (SDF). Subrahmanyam (2007) mentions contingent claims as one of the four central "paradigms" of finance. This mention occurs in his introduction; however, he does not return to the topic in the body of his survey.

None of the other surveys accord the contingent claims approach much emphasis. I regard this deficiency as significant. A major result in neoclassical asset pricing is that in the absence of full arbitrage, all securities can be priced in terms of a single stochastic discount factor (SDF). Yet, in Barberis et al. (2001a), a risky security is priced relative to one SDF, and the default-free security is priced relative to another SDF. This dual structure implies the existence of arbitrage profits. However, Barberis et al. (2001a) do not discuss the issue, either to explain it or to provide some form of justification, behavioral, or otherwise.

It seems to me that behavioralizing the contingent claims approach lies at the heart of behavioralizing finance. In Section 5, I discuss the nature of a behavioral contingent claims approach. This discussion will address two particular topics, sentiment, and the character of a behavioral representative investor.

2.5.4.1 Sentiment

Sentiment is one of the central concepts of behavioral asset pricing. Yet, absent from much of the behavioral asset pricing literature is a coherent definition of sentiment. Instead, sentiment seems to be model-specific. In some models it corresponds to errors in means, in other models errors in probabilities. A good illustration of this point can be found in Shleifer (2000) where the formal treatment of sentiment varies from section to section. The absence of a clear formal definition of sentiment makes it difficult to ask generally how sentiment is manifest in asset prices, and specifically how it impacts the cross-section.

2.5.4.2 Representative Investor

Like their neoclassical counterparts, behavioral asset pricing theorists are prone to build representative investor models. Whereas neoclassical asset pricing theorists build models in which a rational representative investor sets prices, behavioral asset pricing theorists build models in which the representative investor exhibits the behavior traits of individuals, as documented in the psychology literature. However, as I discuss in Section 5, aggregation theory strongly indicates that in the presence of heterogeneous investors, the representative investor will reflect but not share the traits exhibited by individual investors. As a result, economists who use standard representative investor models are prone to "representativeness bias," a common pattern documented in the behavioral decision literature. This statement applies to neoclassical economists working in the tradition of Mehra and Prescott (1985), whose asset pricing model features a representative investor with constant relative risk aversion. Moreover, the statement applies equally to behavioral economists whose models feature representative investors with behavioral beliefs and preferences identified with individuals. Examples include Barberis et al. (1998) and Barberis et al. (2001a).

3

Behavioralizing Beliefs and Preferences

Generally speaking, sentiment reflects the influence of psychology on beliefs and preferences. The focus of the present section is the behavioralization of neoclassical beliefs and preferences.

An excellent discussion of behavioral beliefs and preferences can be found in Fox and See (2003). I draw from some of their discussion as well as Shefrin (2007) to describe how behaviorists have introduced psychological elements into the neoclassical framework.

In neoclassical finance, investor preferences are assumed to obey the axioms of expected utility theory, where the expectation is taken with respect to probability beliefs. In this respect, the expected utility function combines both beliefs (probability distributions) and preferences (utility function). Survey evidence indicates that the proportion of the population whose behavior conforms to expected utility theory is small. See Bruhin et al. (2009a) who suggest a figure of about 20 percent, which provides an indication of the relative importance of developing a coherent behavioral approach.

Expected utility theory models risky prospects as random variables or more generally as stochastic processes. Here each realization $\tilde{x}$ of a random process x generates a utility $u(\tilde{x})$. Expected utility $E[u]$ is the expectation of utility u with respect to the probabilities governing x. A natural question to ask is whether there are behavioral counterparts to the neoclassical notions of utility function, probability distribution, and process of maximization? The purpose of this section is to address this question, with a view toward identifying structure.

3.1 Behavioral Beliefs: Heuristics and Biases

In neoclassical finance, investors' beliefs are typically assumed to be free from bias, meaning that investors' beliefs correspond to the actual probabilities governing x. However, the heuristics and biases literature suggest the presence of systematic biases, thereby leading to distorted beliefs. Some types of phenomena, such as optimism, overconfidence, extrapolation bias, and gambler's fallacy, can all be modeled as biases to the probabilities representing investors' beliefs. However, other phenomena such as ambiguity aversion are inconsistent with beliefs represented as probability densities. I discuss both types of situations below.

The concept "change of measure" is well established in asset pricing theory, where it is commonly used to convert physical (or true) probabilities into risk neutral probabilities. In this section, I discuss how the change of measure approach can also capture the impact of particular psychological biases, relative to neoclassical beliefs.

To illustrate the concept of change of measure, consider a random variable x which is normally distributed $N(0,1)$. The probability density function (pdf) of x is $\frac{1}{\sqrt{2\pi}}e^{-\frac{1}{2}x^2}$. Consider multiplying the pdf of x by a change of measure function $\xi(x) = e^{x\mu-\frac{1}{2}\mu^2}$. Doing so, and grouping terms in the exponent, leads to the function $\frac{1}{\sqrt{2\pi}}e^{-\frac{1}{2}[x-\mu]^2}$. This, of course, is the pdf for a random variable which is normally distributed $N(\mu,1)$. Hence, the operation of multiplying the pdf of x by the change of measure ξ has led to a shift in mean.

Some biases can be modeled as simple shifts in mean. For example, let x be the abnormal return to a security which is normally distributed $N(0,1)$. Interpret the zero mean as the security being fairly priced in the market. An investor who is unrealistically optimistic might believe that the mean of x is $\mu > 0$. In this case, optimism bias can be modeled as a right shift in the mean of x, which is accomplished through a change of measure. On the other hand pessimism bias corresponds to a shift in mean where $\mu < 0$.

By definition, the change of measure function ξ is the ratio of the probability density of the mean-shifted random variable to the probability density of the original random variable. Consider the log-change of measure $ln(\xi)$. The log-change of measure, evaluated at x, effectively measures the percentage difference between the mean-shifted probability and original probability associated with x. In effect, the log-change of measure is a metric for the probability bias associated with each potential realization of x.

Notice that in the mean-shift example above, $ln(\xi)$ is just a linear function of x, $\mu x - \frac{1}{2}\mu^2$. Consider the case of optimism bias, so that $\mu > 0$. For sufficiently low values of x, the log-change of measure will be negative, meaning that probabilities assigned to very negative returns will be too low. For sufficiently high values of x, the log-change of measure will be positive, meaning the probabilities assigned to very positive returns will be too high (Figure 3.1).

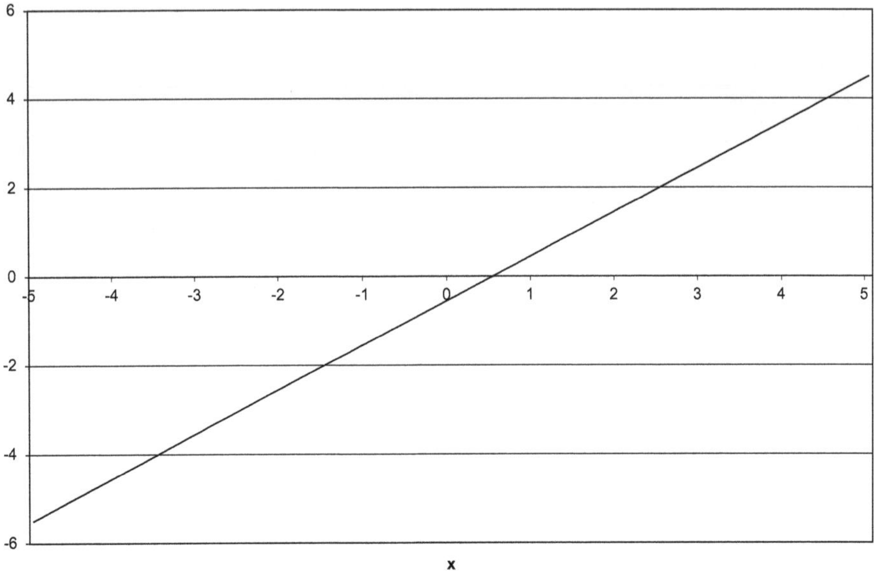

Fig. 3.1 Illustration of a log-change of measure corresponding to optimism bias.

If x is $N(\mu, \sigma)$ then its pdf has the form $\frac{1}{\sqrt{2\pi\sigma^2}} exp(-\frac{(x-\mu)^2}{2\sigma^2})$. Consider two normally distributed random variables x_1 and x_2. The ratio of the pdf of x_2 to the pdf of x_1 provides the change of measure $\xi_{1,2}$ which transforms x_1 into x_2. If x_1 is the true random variable, and x_2 represents an investor's beliefs about this variable, then the log-change of measure $ln(\xi_{1,2})$ is a metric for the investor's probability bias function. If $\sigma_1 \neq \sigma_2$, then the log-change of measure will not be linear in the values of x. For example, suppose that $\mu_1 = \mu_2$ and $\sigma_1 > \sigma_2$. When it comes to tail events, the investor will associate probabilities to these events which are too low. Hence, the log-change of measure will be negative in both the upper tail and the lower tail, but positive in the mid-range. In particular the log-change of measure will have the shape of an inverted-U.

Overconfidence is typically understood to imply that investors underestimate risk. For example, if the true return process is given by x_1 in the preceding paragraph, and an investor believes that the return process is given by x_2, then overconfidence is represented by the condition $\sigma_2 < \sigma_1$. Hence, overconfidence is associated with a log-change of measure whose shape is an inverted-U (Figure 3.2).

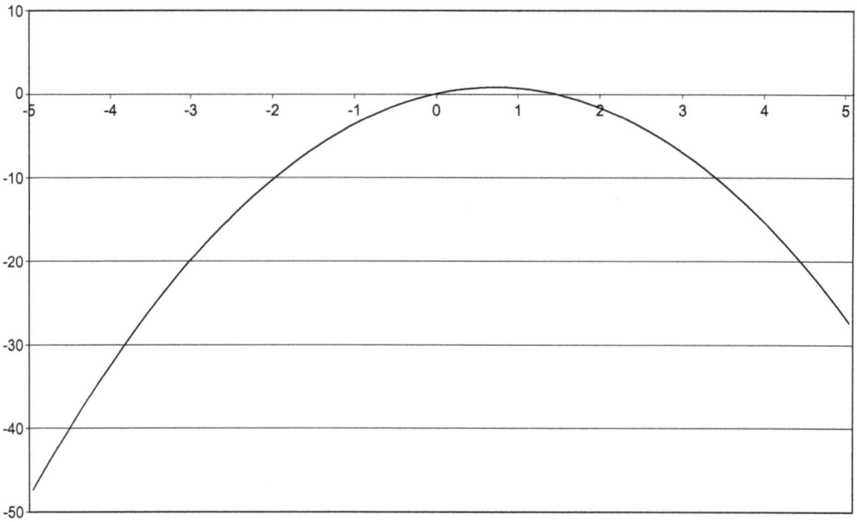

Fig. 3.2 Illustration of a log-change of measure corresponding to overconfidence bias.

Extrapolation bias (also known as "hot hand fallacy") and gambler's fallacy both stem from judgmental heuristics. Notably, both can give rise to time varying optimism and pessimism. These biases are dynamic, referring as they do to biases in conditional probabilities related to a stochastic process. If the recent portion of the realized trajectory features a run of predominantly favorable outcomes, then hot hand fallacy gives rise to excessive optimism, while gambler's fallacy gives rise to excessive pessimism.

Typically, optimism is associated with a shift in mean, whereas overconfidence is associated with a shift in variance. However, hot hand fallacy and gambler's fallacy can also apply to beliefs about variance. Hot hand fallacy predicts that after a recent period of high volatility, subsequent volatility will continue to be high, whereas gambler's fallacy predicts a decline in subsequent volatility.

As was mentioned above, some beliefs are not representable as probabilities. Aversion to ambiguity can be represented in several ways. One way is through the use of Choquet integrals, where decision weights take the place of probabilities and do not integrate to unity over the entire population of possible outcomes (Fox and See, 2003). Notably, the ratio of a Choquet density to a probability density is also a change of measure, transforming a probability density to a Choquet density. Therefore, the change of measure approach applies here as well.

Over time, economists are making increasing use of insights from the psychology literature. An example is support theory, in which probabilities are attached not to events per se, but to descriptions of events (Tversky and Koehler, 1994; Diecidue and La-Ornual, 2009).

3.2 Behavioral Preferences

In expected utility theory, preferences are completely captured by the utility function. In contrast, behavioral preferences are embodied within both the counterpart to a utility function and in decision weights associated with probabilities. In this section I discuss two psychologically based approaches to risk preferences. The first is the cumulative version of prospect theory (CPT), and the second is SP/A theory.

Both theories focus on the cumulative (or decumulative) distribution function, and both involve weighting functions whose shape

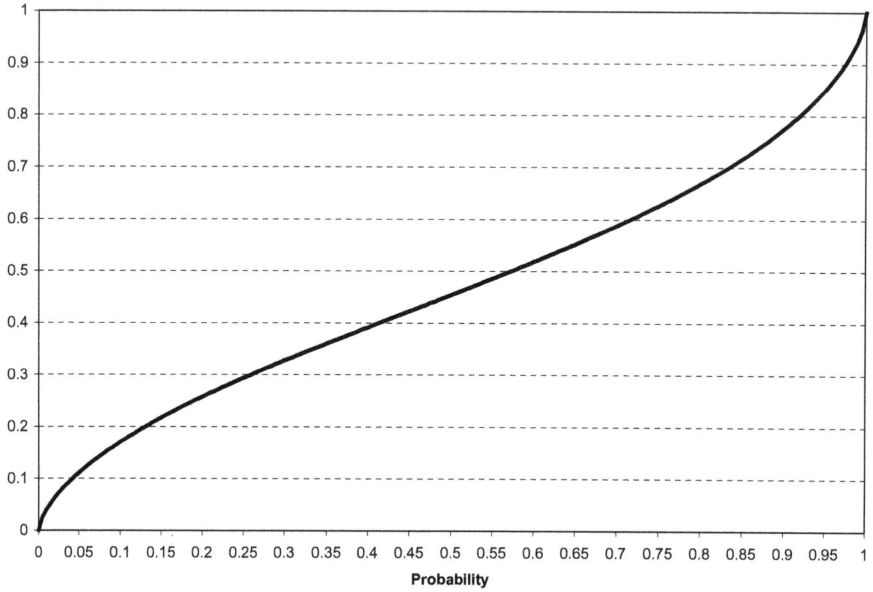

Fig. 3.3 Illustration of a weighting function for decumulative probabilities with an inverse-S shape.

resembles an inverse-S (Figure 3.3). In CPT, the inverse-S shape reflects the principle of diminishing sensitivity, known as "psychophysics." In SP/A theory, the inverse-S shape reflects the impact of emotions, most notably fear and hope. Notably, the inverse-S shaped weighting function gives rise to a U-shaped log-change of measure in which probabilities of extreme events are overweighted and probabilities of intermediate events are underweighted.

To introduce some notation, denote the set of possible outcomes by a finite set of real numbers $X = \{x_1, \dots x_n\}$, ordered from the lowest outcome x_1 to the highest x_n. Formally, a risky alternative or prospect is a random variable that takes on values in X. One way to describe the probabilities attached to a random variable is to use a decumulative distribution function D, where $D(x)$ is the probability that the outcome payoff is at least x. The same probabilistic information is also conveyed by the cumulative distribution function, which measures the probability that the outcome payoff is no greater than x, or the probability density function which measures the probability that the outcome payoff is exactly x.

3.2.1 Prospect Theory

Prospect theory is a theory of choice developed by psychologists Daniel Kahneman and Amos Tversky (Kahneman and Tversky, 1979; Tversky and Kahneman, 1992).[1] Prospect theory has four distinctive features. First, the carriers of utility are changes, meaning gains and losses relative to a reference point, not final position.

Second, the utility function (known as a value function in prospect theory) is concave in gains and concave in losses, typically with a point of nondifferentiability at the origin so that the function is more steeply sloped for losses (to the left of the origin) than for gains (to the right of the origin) (Figure 3.4). Hence, the utility function is S-shaped with a kink at the origin. Tversky and Kahneman (1992) suggest using

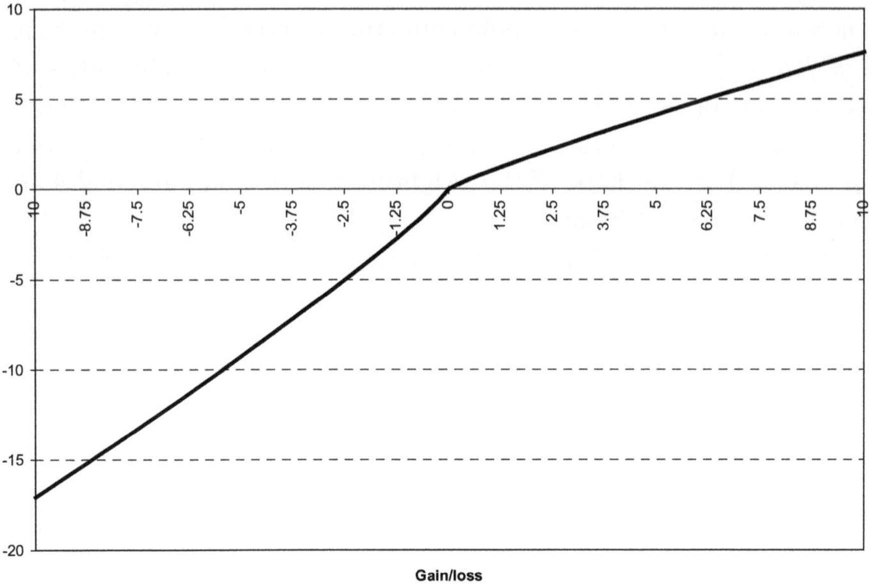

Fig. 3.4 Illustration of an S-shaped value function.

[1] See Wang et al. (2009) for a survey-based analysis of cross-country differences in responses to prospect theoretic questions.

a utility function $u(x)$ with the form x^{α} in the domain of gains ($x \geq 0$) and $-\lambda(-x)^{\beta}$ in the domain of losses ($x \leq 0$).[2]

Third, probabilities are weighted (or distorted) when prospects are evaluated. In the original 1979 version of prospect theory (OPT), the weighting function π has probability density p as its argument. The π-function in OPT is convex, with $\pi(p) > p$ for small positive values of p and $\pi(p) < p$ for high values of p less than 1. Tversky and Kahneman (1992) proposed a cumulative version of prospect theory (CPT) that uses rank-dependent utility. Unlike OPT, where probability weights depend only on probability density, the weights in CPT depend on outcome rank.

Tversky and Kahneman (1992) use two weighting functions, one function for gains and one function for losses. Both functions take decumulative probabilities as their arguments, where the decumulative distribution pertains to the absolute value of the gain or loss, respectively. The weighting function is similar to the h-transform used by Lopes. It features an inverse S-shape, which Tversky–Kahneman generate using the ratio of a power function to a Hölder average; that is, $p^{\gamma}/(p^{\gamma} + (1-p)^{\gamma})^{1/\gamma}$. As a result, in CPT it is the probabilities of extreme outcomes that are overweighted (very large losses and very large gains). As I mentioned in the previous section, Ingersoll (2008) points out that the shape of the weighting function only resembles an inverse-S for part of its range.

Both the S-shape of the utility function and the inverse S-shape of the weighting functions reflect psychophysics, meaning the diminished sensitivity to successive changes. For the utility function, the changes pertain to differences relative to the reference point. For the weighting function, the changes pertain to differences relative to the endpoints 0 and 1.

Fourth, decision makers engage in editing or framing before formally evaluating risky prospects. There are several types of editing issues. Perhaps, the simplest editing issue is the choice of reference point.

[2] Strictly speaking, the first derivatives of these functions at zero approach infinity, and therefore do not display a kink. However, a suitably small translation of both functions leads the first derivatives to be finite at zero, with the kink in question.

Kahneman and Tversky illustrate this issue by describing a medical task in which the data can be presented, or framed, in one of two ways. The first way is in terms of lives saved, while the second way is in terms of lives lost. The "lives saved" frame implicitly sets the reference point at 100 percent fatalities. The "lives lost" frame implicitly sets the reference point at 0 percent fatalities. Although the data underlying the two frames are identical, physicians tend to act as if they are more risk averse when presented with the data framed in terms of "lives saved" than when the data are framed in terms of "lives lost." This choice pattern is consistent with the S-shaped utility function.

A more complex framing issues is the segmentation of a complicated decision task into a series of subtasks. The structure of each subtask is called a "mental account" and the segmentation process is known as "narrow framing." Because narrow framing tends to overlook interdependencies between mental accounting structures, the segmentation process is often suboptimal. Tversky and Kahneman present examples in which narrow framing leads to the selection of stochastically dominated choices. Prospect theory is a descriptive framework, not a normative framework. People who choose stochastically dominated alternatives do so because they do not always grasp the complete structure of the decision tasks they confront. The complete structure is typically opaque, not transparent, and people lack the ability to frame complex decision tasks transparently.

3.2.2 SP/A Theory

Lopes (1987) and Lopes and Oden (1999) developed a psychologically based approach known as SP/A theory to explain choice among risky alternatives. Lopes titled her 1987 article "The Psychology of Risk: Between Hope and Fear" to capture the idea that the emotions of hope and fear play key roles in choice among risky alternatives. In this respect, the letters that make up SP/A refer to specific concepts which measure or impact the degree of fear or hope experienced by a decision maker. Notably, S stands for "security," P stands for "potential," and A stands for "aspiration."

In a typical decision task, a decision maker chooses a best alternative from a menu $\{D\}$ of risky alternatives. The role of the theory is to describe the criteria leading to the choice. In SP/A theory, risky alternatives are evaluated using an objective function whose arguments reflect security S, potential P, and aspiration A. See Diecidue and van de Ven (2008) and Bruhin et al. (2009b) for some recent treatments of the role of aspiration in economic choice. Payne (2005) describes an experiment whose results suggest that because of aspiration, SP/A theory better predicts choice than prospect theory.

Roughly speaking, increased fear stems from reduced security, and reduced security corresponds to an increase in the probability attached to the occurrence of some unfavorable event. Suppose we consider two decision makers who face an identical risk, or prospect D, but experience different degrees of fear. Intuitively, the decision maker who experiences more fear attaches greater importance to the probability associated with unfavorable events than the decision maker who experiences less fear.

Formally, Lopes uses rank-dependent utility to capture the effects of fear. In rank-dependent utility, a decision maker who faced a risky prospect D acts as if the decumulative density function is the transform $h(D)$ rather than D itself. In SP/A theory, fear operates on the probabilities associated with unfavorable events. Because D is a decumulative distribution function, the probability attached to the least favorable event x_1 is given by $\text{Prob}\{x_1\} = D(x_1) - D(x_2)$.

Under the transform $h(D)$, the probability attached to the least favorable event x_1 is given by $\text{Prob}\{x_1\} = h(D(x_1)) - h(D(x_2))$. In Lopes' framework, a decision maker who is fearful about exposure to event x_1 overweights the probability attached to x_1. That is, the fearful decision maker employs a transform h which satisfies:

$$h(D(x_1)) - h(D(x_2)) > D(x_1) - D(x_2). \tag{3.1}$$

Because x_1 is the least favorable outcome, the probability that the actual outcome turns out to be x_1 or higher is 1. In other words, $D(x_1) = 1$. What Equation (3.1) effectively states is that increased fear leads to an increase in the slope of the h-function in the neighborhood of 1.

Rank-dependent utility also captures the manner in which the decision maker experiences hope. Hope is associated with upside potential, or potential for short. Hope induces a decision maker to attach greater weight to the most favorable events. Because D is a decumulative distribution function, the probability attached to the most favorable event x_n is given by $\text{Prob}\{x_n\} = D(x_n)$. Therefore, the emotion of hope leads a decision maker to employ a transform h which satisfies $h(D(x_n)) > D(x_n)$. For the second most favorable outcome, the corresponding inequality would read:

$$h(D(x_n)) - h(D(x_{n-1})) > D(x_n) - D(x_{n-1}). \tag{3.2}$$

This inequality indicates that increased hope leads to an increase in the slope of the h-function in the neighborhood of 0.

In Lopes' framework, a person who neither experiences fear nor hope is associated with an h-function that is the identify function: $h(D) = D$. A decision maker who experiences only fear, but not hope, is associated with an h-function that is strictly convex in D: it is steep in the neighborhood of 1 and flat in the neighborhood of 0. Formally, Lopes uses a power function $h_S(D) = D^q$, $q > 1$ for this case. A decision maker who experiences only hope is associated with an h-function that is strictly concave in D. Formally, Lopes uses a power function $h_P(D) = 1 - (1 - D)^p$, $p > 1$ for this case. A person who experiences both fear and hope is associated with an h-function that has an inverse-S shape. It is concave in the neighborhood of the origin and convex in the neighborhood of 1. Formally, Lopes uses a convex combination of the power functions h_S and h_P to capture this case (Figure 3.5).

In SP/A theory, the degree to which fear and hope are experienced depends on the degree to which risky prospects offer security S and potential P. To capture the impact of both security and potential, Lopes uses an expected utility function with probabilities derived from the h-transform. She calls the function SP for security-potential, and it has the form:

$$SP = \sum_{i=1}^{n} (h(D_i) - h(D_{i+1}))u(x_i). \tag{3.3}$$

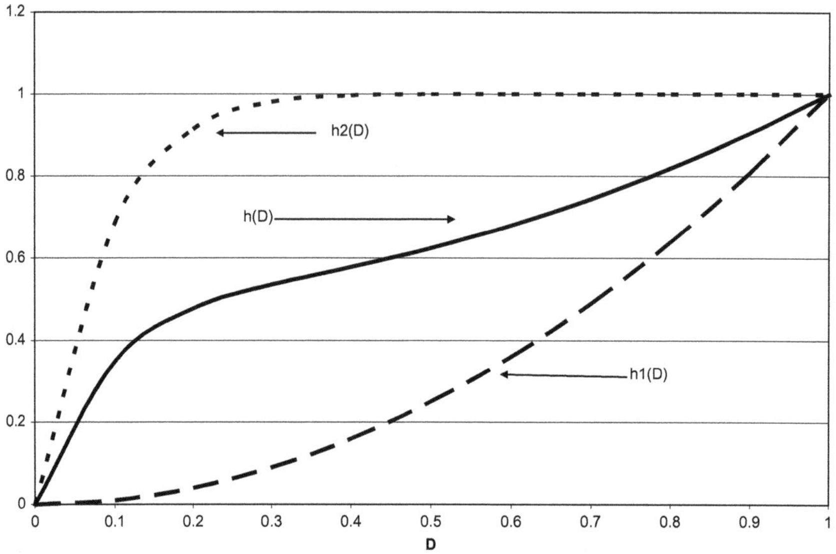

Fig. 3.5 Illustration of three decumulative transformation functions in Lopes' SP/A framework.

In Equation (4.1), u is a utility function whose argument is outcome x. Although Lopes uses the assumption $u(x) = x$ in most of her analysis, Lopes and Oden (1999) comment that in practice, u might display a bit of concavity.

The "A" in SP/A denotes aspiration. Aspiration pertains to a target value α (or range) to which the decision maker aspires. Aspiration points reflect different types of goals. For example, a decision maker might wish to generate an outcome that would allow the purchase of a particular good or service. Alternatively, the aspiration point might reflect a status quo position that corresponds to the notion of no gain or loss. In Lopes' framework, aspiration-risk is measured as the probability $A = Prob\{x \geq \alpha\}$ that the random outcome x meets or exceeds the aspiration level α.

In SP/A theory, the decision maker maximizes an objective function $V(SP, A)$ in deciding which alternative D to choose from the menu of available prospects. V is strictly monotone increasing in both of its arguments. Therefore, there are situations in which a decision maker is willing to trade off some SP in exchange for a higher value of A.

3.3 Regret

In the early development of prospect theory, Kahneman and Tversky focused on the role of regret. Regret is the psychological pain associated with recognizing after the fact that taking a different decision would have produced a better outcome. Kahneman and Tversky eventually built prospect theory using the S-shaped value function, but in Kahneman and Tversky (1982) continued to emphasize the importance of regret. They pointed out that regret will be magnified by the ease with which a person can easily imagine taking a different decision. In consequence, regret avoidance discourages deviations from behavior viewed as conventional, a version of status quo bias.

The volume edited by Loomes and Sugden (1982) contains a formal treatment of decision making when preferences are determined by regret. Shefrin and Statman (1984, 1985) modify the concept of regret to reflect pride in the domain of gains. Gollier and Salanié (2006) develop a regret-based model to analyze the character of the risk premium in an asset pricing model.

3.4 Self-Control

Self-control refers to situations when a person is conflicted, and thinks he or she should take one decision, but emotionally feels like taking a different decision. Studies of self-control in financial economics tend to emphasize the difficulty in delaying gratification. However, self-control applies more broadly, and in particular applies when the emotion of regret prevents a person from taking a decision that they "think" is appropriate.

Shefrin and Thaler (1988) extend the neoclassical life cycle framework to incorporate psychological elements associated with self-control and editing. The behavioral life cycle framework features a two-self framework focused on the interaction between a person's rational self (a "planner" corresponding to activity in the prefrontal cortex of the brain) and an impulsive self (a "doer" corresponding to activity in the limbic system of the brain). In addition to traditional neoclassical variables such as consumption, the behavioral life cycle framework adds psychological variables to represent "temptation," "willpower," "rules," and associated psychological costs for exhibiting self-control. In particular, rules are represented by constraints which resemble corner solutions. People may choose to violate a rule they themselves establish, but doing so entails a psychological cost.

When the work of Shefrin and Thaler (1988) was published, the field of neuroeconomics was nonexistent. However, neuroeconomics is now flourishing, and providing neurological support for psychologically based models. For example, Hare et al. (2009) identify a specific region in the prefrontal cortex associated with self-control, the DLPFC. Knutson et al. (2008) identify hope with a region of the brain called the nucleus accumbens. Knoch et al. (2009) study the impact of breakdowns in prefrontal cortex activity on reputation. With advances in neuroeconomics, economists are beginning to develop sophisticated models of brain activity (Brocas and Carrillo, 2008).

4

Behavioralizing Portfolio Selection Theory

In their survey article, Barberis and Thaler (2003) identify empirical features characterizing portfolio selection by individual investors. These include the following:

— lack of diversification associated with the $1/n$-heuristic,
— home bias associated with familiarity and ambiguity aversion,
— excessive trading associated with overconfidence,
— the disposition effect associated with prospect theory, regret, and self-control
— the attention hypothesis associated with availability bias, and
— dividends associated with self-control.

In this section, I focus attention on the following series of additional issues:

— desire for positively skewed returns,
— role of dividends as a self-control device and managing risk, and
— status quo bias.

The sheer number of effects, most at odds with the neoclassical mean-variance approach, indicates that the behavioralization of portfolio theory will be very rich. At present, it is also a work in progress.[1] The purpose of this section is to describe the implications of some of the behavioral preference frameworks for portfolio selection, and relate these to empirical evidence.

A broad issue that arises in this section concerns the role of optimization. A first step in the behavioralization of portfolio theory is to replace neoclassical preferences with behavioral preferences and undertake a full maximization. Doing so yields some interesting insights. However, there is ample evidence that individual investors are imperfect maximizers. Therefore, the issues described in this section begin with full maximization and then move on to quasi-maximization.

4.1 Preference for Positively Skewed Returns: Full Maximization

4.1.1 Empirical Issues

In contrast to neoclassical portfolio theory, which emphasizes mean-variance efficiency, behavioral portfolio theory emphasizes the taste for positive skewness. There is strong evidence that people have a taste for positively skewed returns. In 2009, LaFleur's magazine reported that the average household in Massachusetts spends $1,760 annually on lotteries, roughly one-third more than the average annual contribution Americans make to their 401(k) plans. The desire for positively skewed returns is related to thrill-seeking. Grinblatt and Keloharju (2009) use a clever database to study thrill-seeking behavior by investors.

A good example of a security with a lottery feature is the British Premium Bond. The Premium Bond was launched by the U.K. government in 1956, and is issued by National Savings and Investments, a government department. Any British citizen can purchase Premium Bonds, with the minimum investment being £100, or with a monthly standing order, £50. The maximum amount a person can invest is £30,000. As with a regular bond, the Premium Bond returns principal on a nominal basis. However, in lieu of monthly interest, investors'

[1] Investor preferences also reflect concerns other than returns, such as social responsibility (Statman, 2008).

returns are determined by a lottery, and moreover are tax-free. For each single pound invested, there is one chance to win. Lobe and Hölzl (2008) document the degree of popularity of this security. The fraction of the U.K. population which invests in Premium Bonds grew from approximately 12 percent in 1957 to 40 percent in 2005. During the 1980s, approximately 45 percent of the population invested in Premium Bonds. Lobe and Hölzl (2008) points out that the tax advantage of Premium Bonds suggests that there are neoclassical reasons to justify why higher income investors would choose to hold Premium Bonds. However, for lower income investors, the attractiveness of these securities is more likely to lie with the manner in which the bonds package safety of principal with the lottery feature of coupon payments.

Statman (2002) and Kumar (2009) investigate the extent to which individual investors hold stocks with lottery-like characteristics. Kumar notes that lotteries offer a low probability of a high payoff (positive skewness), feature low prices per ticket, and have negative expected returns. Similarly, lottery-like stocks feature positively skewed return distributions, low prices per share, and possibly negative expected returns.

After classifying stocks into lottery stocks and non-lottery stocks, Kumar compares the portfolio weights individual investors assign to lottery stocks to both a random assignment as well as the portfolio weights institutional investors assign to lottery stocks. A random assignment would allocate 0.74 percent of the portfolio to lottery stocks. On average, individual investors allocate 8.3 percent of their portfolios to lottery stocks. Kumar also reports that even the most wealthy individual investors allocate 7.7 percent of their portfolios to lottery stocks. In contrast, institutional investors allocate 0.28 percent of their portfolios to lottery stocks.

At the opposite end of the spectrum lie stocks that are the mirror images of lottery stocks. These stocks feature low volatility, are less positively skewed, have higher prices per share, and higher expected returns. The random assignment would allocate 54 percent of a portfolio to stocks that are diametrically opposite to lottery stocks. The weight assigned by individual investors is 33 percent, and the weight assigned by institutional investors is 59 percent.

Polkovnichenko (2002) reports that the wealthiest group of investors hold almost the same amount in direct equity as indirect equity. Similarly, Kumar reports that investors who hold larger mutual fund portfolios invest more in lottery stocks. Kumar also finds that the highest turnover is among buyers of lottery stocks.

In line with risk-seeking behavior in the domain of losses, Kumar finds that when economic conditions deteriorate, people increase their allocations to lottery stocks. In particular, he finds that on a risk-adjusted basis, those who invest in lottery stocks earn 5.9 percent a year less than those who do not. Those who invest heavily in lottery stocks earn 8.9 percent less than those who invest moderately in lottery stocks. The 8.9 percent actually corresponds to 13.1 percent on a risk-adjusted basis.

4.1.2 Theoretical Issues

Consider the traditional Markowitz portfolio selection problem when security returns are normally distributed. Formally, let w is a vector of portfolio weights, Σ be a return covariance matrix, R be a vector of expected returns, and $\tau \in [0, \infty)$ measure the degree of risk tolerance. Then the mean-variance efficient frontier is the family of solutions to the w-minimization of $w^T \Sigma w - \tau R^T w$, for varying τ. Associated with each mean-variance portfolio is a normally distributed return distribution.

A key feature of the mean-variance efficient portfolios is the two-fund separation property. In this case, any mean-variance efficient portfolio is a convex combination of a unique risky portfolio and the risk-free portfolio.

4.1.2.1 Full Maximization with Behavioral Preferences

The starting point for behavioralizing portfolio theory involves the replacement of a mean-variance objective function with a behavioral objective function in the optimization procedure. The two main objective functions used in the literature are the prospect theory weighting function $\sum W_i v(x_i)$ and the SP/A function $V(SP, A)$.

Consider how different an optimized behavioral portfolio return distribution is from a mean-variance return distribution. To describe the

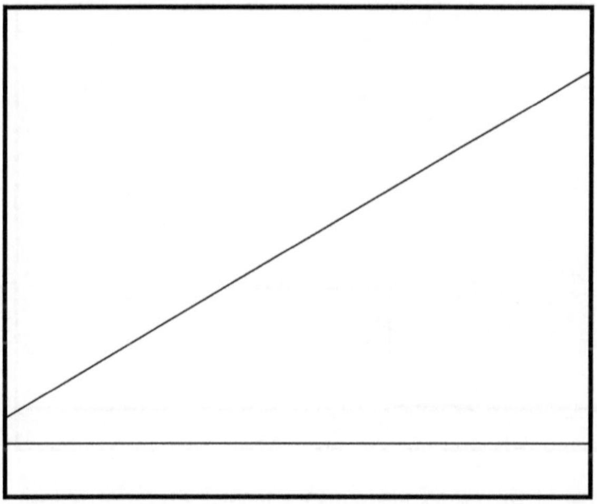

Fig. 4.1 Illustration of the payoff pattern to the risk-free security and a combination of the risk-free security and unique mean-variance risky security. The x-axis is the gross return to the unique risky mean-variance security.

contrast, consider a series of graphs with the return to the unique risky mean-variance portfolio on the x-axis. Figure 4.1 illustrates the returns to two portfolios relative to the unique risky portfolio. One of the two portfolios is risk-free, returning the risk-free rate, and the other combines the risk-free security and the unique risky security.

Figure 4.2 illustrates the return to a behavioral portfolio associated with prospect theory preferences when the weighting function is the identity function, meaning the weights are themselves probabilities. Notice that the returns to loss states are very low, and in fact are associated with a lower bound on achievable return. This boundary property stems from the fact that the value function is convex in the domain of losses. The kink at the origin of the value function, in combination with subcertainty, can produce a flat region with neither gain nor loss. In the domain of gains, the behavioral return is similar to a neoclassical return, as the value function is concave in gains. See also Barberis and Huang (2008).

Figure 4.3 illustrates the possible impact of the weighting function in the domain of gains. With overweighting of probabilities at the extremes, the behavioral return distribution corresponds to an inverse-S

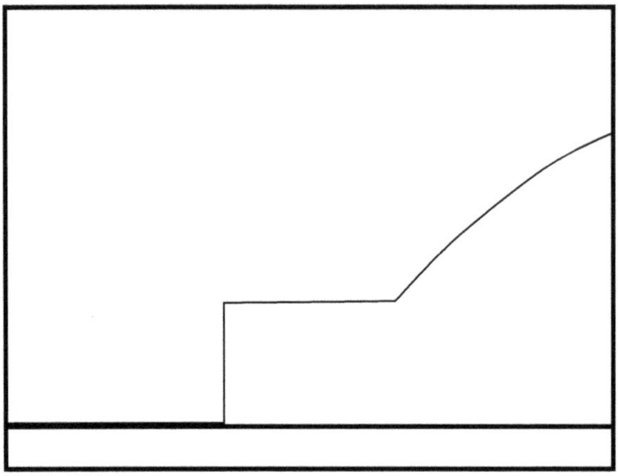

Fig. 4.2 Illustration of the payoff pattern to a portfolio associated with optimization of a prospect theory criterion function with probabilities as weights. The x-axis is the gross return to the unique risky mean-variance security.

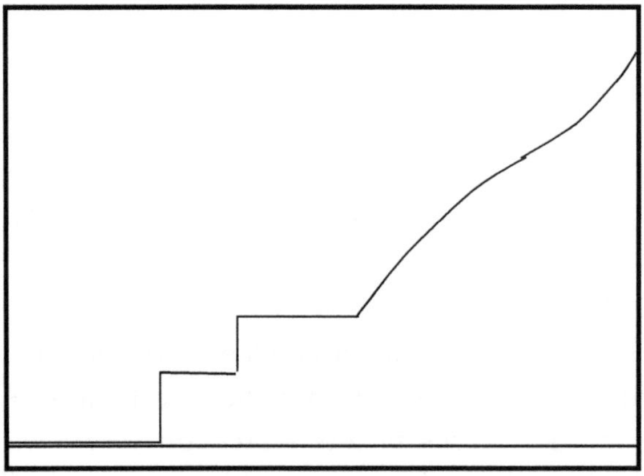

Fig. 4.3 Illustration of the payoff pattern to a portfolio associated with optimization of a prospect theory criterion function with an inverse-S-shaped weighting function. The x-axis is the gross return to the unique risky mean-variance security.

in the domain of gains. This occurs because the probabilities associated with intermediate gains tend to be underweighted, whereas the probabilities associated with extreme gains tend to be overweighted, thereby giving rise to positive skewness, in that there is a small probability of an especially large gain.

Notably, the weighting function is rank dependent, thereby introducing kinks into the indifference map. For losses, overweighting of extreme loss probabilities can introduce a convex feature that operates in the opposite direction from the shape of the value function in the domain of losses. In the domain of gains, the overweighting of extreme gain probabilities introduces a non-convex feature that operates in the opposite direction from the shape of the value function in the domain of gains. The effect of probability weighting can produce a non-boundary flat return in the domain of losses, and accentuated risk seeking in the domain of gains.

Prospect theory portfolios tend to feature either boundary solutions or unbounded solutions, a feature noted in the early drafts of Shefrin and Statman (2000), and explored more fully in Shefrin (2008a). See also De Giorgi et al. (2009) and He and Zhou (2009). He and Zhou call this an "ill posed problem."

The early versions of Shefrin and Statman (2000) used prospect theory as the basis for a behavioral portfolio theory. In commenting on these drafts, Daniel Kahneman suggested to Statman and me that Lopes' SP/A theory might provide a superior approach to CPT. The published version of Shefrin and Statman (2000) develops an SP/A-based behavioral portfolio selection theory, emphasizing the roles of fear, hope, and aspiration. See Diecidue and van de Ven (2008) and De Giorgi (2009) who focus on the impact of aspiration on portfolio returns.

Figure 4.4 illustrates the contrast between a typical SP/A-based portfolio return and the risky mean-variance return. Notice that the SP/A return function has three segments. Begin with the middle segment. It is flat and the return corresponds to the achievement of the aspiration level. To the left is a region where the investor fails to achieve the aspiration level. With concave utility, and in the absence of probability weighting, this region will typically be strictly concave and increasing. Probability weighting tends to flatten this region, perhaps to the point of rendering it completely flat as depicted in the figure. With linear utility, this region will lie on the boundary. At the right is a region where the investor achieves a return above aspiration. Depending on the utility function and specific parameters, one or more of these

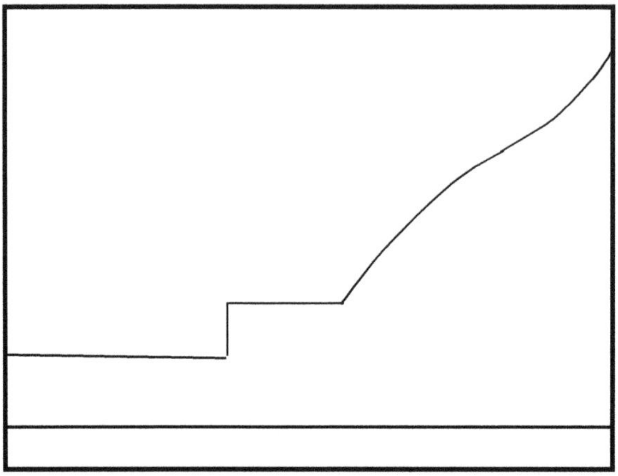

Fig. 4.4 Illustration of the payoff pattern to a portfolio associated with optimization of an SP/A criterion function with an inverse-S-shaped weighting function. The x-axis is the gross return to the unique risky mean-variance security.

regions might disappear. Because of probability weighting, the return pattern typically has the shape of an inverse-S. With concave utility, and absent probability weighting, the shape is typically concave and increasing. With linear utility, the region is very small, but features a spike at the highest return.

Recall the discussion in Section 3 concerning the use of change of measure to model behavioral beliefs. In this regard, the various behavioral return patterns below can be expressed as expected utility maximizing solutions, relative to a change of measure. To see why, let equilibrium state prices be given by ν. Begin with the equilibrium consumption profile c_S chosen by an investor with SP/A preferences based on utility function u. Now ask whether we can identify a probability density function P^* such that an expected utility maximizing investor with utility function u and beliefs P^* would have selected c_S?

Let i and k be two states. For equilibrium prices ν, choose P_i^* and P_k^* such that:

$$P_i^* u_i / P_k^* u_k = \nu_i / \nu_k, \tag{4.1}$$

where u_i and u_k are marginal utilities of consumption evaluated at c_S. Then, normalize so that the components P^* sum to unity.

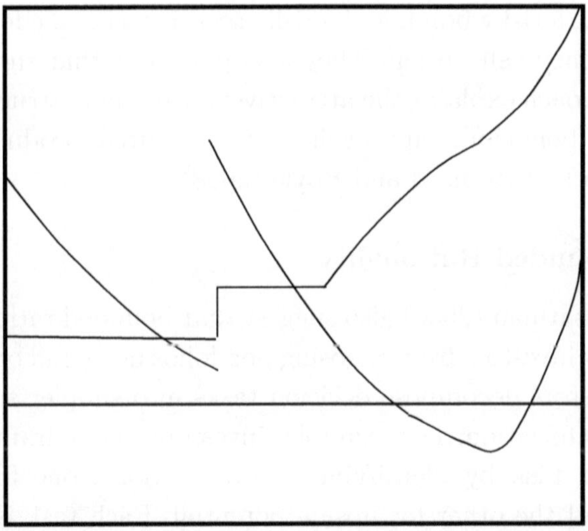

Fig. 4.5 Illustration of the change of measure associated with the payoff pattern to a portfolio associated with optimization of an SP/A criterion function with an inverse-S-shaped weighting function. The x-axis is the gross return to the unique risky mean-variance security.

If Π denotes the objective probability density function, then the function $L = ln(P^*/\Pi)$ is a log-change of measure that captures the impact of the SP/A investor's behavioral preferences and behavioral beliefs. For example, Figure 4.5 adds a stylized change of measure to Figure 4.4. Notice that the pattern can be constructed by beginning with a U-like shape, corresponding to the change of measure associated with the inverse-S shaped weighting function in SP/A theory. The U-shape reflects the fact that the probabilities of extreme events are overweighted and intermediate events are underweighted. In Figure 4.5, the right side of the U is weaker than the left side. Notice that the middle section features a jump at the discontinuity marking the boundary of the middle region, typically followed by a decline to reflect the fact that the behavioral portfolio return is flat at the aspiration point, whereas expected utility maximization typically calls for an increasing return profile.

Shefrin and Statman (2000) point out that SP/A-based portfolio theory provides a rationale for the attractiveness of securities like the Premium Bond. An SP/A portfolio combines safety in the form of a risk-free bond, a risky bond, and a risky security with the features of an out-of-the-money call option. They also point out that the behavioral portfolio approach explains the attractiveness of many structured products. Recent behavioral approaches to structured products includes Rieger (2008) and Bernard and Boyle (2008).

4.1.2.2 Bounded Rationality

Shefrin and Statman (2000) also suggest that bounded rationality typically prevents investors from choosing portfolios using full optimization. Instead, investors decompose decision tasks into simpler sub-task and use quasi-optimization. For example, investors might frame the portfolio selection task by identifying two aspirations, one for downside protection and the other for upside potential. Each task is associated with its own mental account and aspiration point. The downside protection account features a low aspiration level (avoiding poverty) and a high probability of achieving this level. The upside potential account features a high aspiration (riches), and a low or modest probability of achieving this aspiration level. In their model, the investor establishes a nonnegative allocation $w = (w_D, w_U)$, $w_D + w_U = 1$, which gives rise to sub-utilities (V_D, V_U), respectively. An allocation w is evaluated using a criterion function $F(V_D, V_U)$, with the portfolio decision being to solve $max_w F$. Shefrin and Statman call such a portfolio a "layered pyramid." By its nature, mental accounting gives rise to incomplete diversification, as investors ignore covariance relationships.

Although this section has emphasized preferences without regard to biased beliefs, be aware that the impact of probability weighting is similar to the impact of biased beliefs.

4.2 Quasi-Maximization

The disposition effect, attention hypothesis, favoring of dividend-paying stocks, status quo bias, and the propensity to trade are all symptoms of bounded rationality. It seems to me that modeling bounded rationality can be more difficult than modeling full rationality. In this respect, behavioral portfolio models can be delicate. For example, Barberis and Huang (2008) develop a dynamic prospect theory model to study the disposition effect. In this regard, they use static theory to identify the solution, and then recast the model in a dynamic context. What they find is that prospect theory can lead investors to sell their losers and purchase more of their winners, in apparent contradiction of the disposition effect. This is an interesting result, which supports the original contention in Shefrin and Statman (1985) that the disposition effect is likely driven by several psychological features, such as mental accounting, regret, and self-control. As I mentioned in Section 2, prospect theory value function, by itself, cannot explain the disposition effect.

Results like those in Barberis and Xiong (2009), together with the ill posed property of prospect theory-based portfolios, suggest that extreme caution is necessary in developing models to capture behavioral portfolio selection.

4.2.1 Empirical Issues

Section 2 covers many of the key empirical findings about individual investors' portfolios. In this section, I focus on issues which emphasize mental accounting issues in a dynamic environment, such as diversification, the disposition effect, cash dividends, and options. Below I offer a few brief comments about diversification and the disposition effect, and then concentrate on cash dividends and options.

Goetzmann and Kumar (2008) document the existence of skilled investors who hold concentrated portfolios. They point out that as investors increase the number of stocks in their portfolios, they tend to choose stocks which co-move, thereby depriving themselves of the benefits of diversification. They also report that older investors have better diversified portfolios and trade less aggressively than their younger counterparts. See also Dorn and Huberman (2005).

Feng and Seasholes (2005) find that susceptibility to the disposition effect declines by 72 percent with sophistication and experience, especially in connection with riding losers. Their finding provides an indication that some investors learn to achieve increased self-control. Seru et al. (2009) report a similar pattern, with the disposition of the median investor improving by 4 percent after a year of trading experience. In respect to regret, Lehenkari (2008) uses Finnish data to provide intriguing evidence that investors are more prone to the disposition effect for stocks they purchased than for stocks they received as gifts or as part of an inheritance. Recent experimental evidence by Fogel and Berry (2006) strongly supports the importance of regret in explaining the disposition effect.

4.2.1.1 Cash Dividends

The first paper in behavioral finance written by economists is Shefrin and Statman (1984). They develop a behavioral explanation for why some investors framework find cash dividends attractive. Their approach emphasizes the roles of self-control, mental accounting, hedonic editing, and regret. Self-control and mental accounting suggest several hypotheses linking consumption and dividends, along with a clientele effect. The theory suggests that older, retired investors rely on a heuristic in which they finance consumption out of an income mental account, but are reluctant to "dip into capital" which resides in an asset mental account. Hedonic editing and regret suggest a connection between stock market movements and dividends. In particular, investors might prefer to finance consumption out of dividends than out of capital in order to avoid the regret of selling off stock which subsequently appreciates by a large amount. About 20 years after being proposed, most of these hypotheses have come to be tested, with the overall results being supportive of the behavioral approach.[2]

Graham and Kumar (2006) measure the preference for dividends by portfolio dividend yield. They report that irrespective of income, older households prefer dividend-paying stocks over non-dividend-paying stocks. For younger households, those with low income exhibit a somewhat stronger preference for dividend-paying stocks than households with higher income. Moreover, the preference for dividends is relatively stable, with dividend yields of individual investors' portfolios changing slowly over time. These findings support the predictions of behavioral dividend theory about the impact of age and income.

[2] The material in this section is taken from Shefrin (2008b).

In terms of stock selection, Graham and Kumar report that older, retired investors hold about 80 percent of their portfolios in dividend-paying stocks, while younger investors hold about 65 percent of their portfolios in dividend-paying stocks. In particular, older investors with low incomes attach more weight to utility stocks than do younger investors with high incomes. The reverse is true for the stocks of firms in the "computers" and "business services" industries. This pattern is consistent with the idea that older, low-income investors focus more on industries with a reputation for paying higher dividends.

Further support for dividend clienteles stems from Graham and Kumar's analysis of household trading behavior. They report that households trade around dividend events such as ex-dividend days, dividend announcement dates, and dividend initiations. Before the ex-dividend date, households that are older or have less income are net buyers of stock. These households also increase their holdings after dividend initiations and exhibit abnormal buying behavior after dividend announcements. These behavior patterns appear to affect the prices for the stocks of small firms, where individual investors' trades play an especially important role.

Consistent with the predictions of behavioral dividend theory, retirement status increases the demand for dividends. Graham and Kumar regress portfolio yield on a series of variables including age and a retirement status dummy. They report that the age variable has a positive and significant coefficient estimate, as does a dummy for retirement status.

Dong et al. (2005) develop panel data from a survey of individual investors in the Netherlands. On a weekly basis, their survey asked questions about personal finance and consumption matters. Of the 2,035 survey respondents, 555 own or previously owned shares in exchange-listed companies or investment funds. Of these investors, less than 20 percent own individual stocks. Also, 40 percent of the investors are at least 55 years of age and 20 percent are at least 65 years of age.

Consistent with the findings of Graham and Kumar (2006) and Baker et al. (2007a), Dong et al. (2005) find that consumption from dividends is confined to investors who are either older or have low incomes.

Outside this group, individual investors do not consume a large portion of their dividends but instead re-invest their dividend income. In contrast to the findings reported by Baker et al., they find that the propensity to consume from dividend income is less than from regular income. Dong et al. (2005) assert that the findings described previously run counter to the behavioral predictions from Shefrin and Statman (1984). However, as pointed out earlier, behavioral theory does not predict that all households consume dividends. Instead, behavioral theory only predicts that older, retired households and low-income households favor dividend-paying stocks to finance consumption. Younger investors with moderate to high incomes have little need to finance consumption with dividends.

According to Dong et al. (2005), their findings support the behavioral prediction for stock dividends. They find that in cases where firms cannot pay a cash dividend, investors indicate that they would prefer companies to pay a stock dividend, as opposed to no dividends. This is a framing effect, because stock dividends involve costs but do not increase the fundamental value of investors' positions. As Dong et al. (p. 124) indicate, "in principle stock dividends are no more than stock splits."

Baker et al. (2007a) provide the strongest evidence for a connection between consumption and dividends. Their analysis makes use of two types of data sets: the Consumer Expenditure Survey (CEX) from the Bureau of Labor Statistics and brokerage account data. The CEX provides panel data on household consumption, income, wealth, dividends, and demographic information. The brokerage data provide information about how individual investors behave when they receive dividends.

The CEX data used by Baker et al. (2007a) cover the period 1988–2001 and involve 3,272 household-year observations. Total expenditure including durables is about $50,000 (measured in December 2001 in dollars). Total income, which includes dividends but not capital gains, has a mean of $56,789. Financial wealth is typically around a third of total wealth. For the mean household, interest income is $1,207 and dividend income is $891. On average, interest and dividends account for 4 percent and 2 percent of total income, respectively. The distribution is skewed, with the median household reporting zero dividend income.

The BLC predicts that the marginal propensity to consume from the income mental account exceeds the marginal propensity to consume from the asset mental account. Shefrin and Statman (1984) suggest that dividends flow through the income mental account and that capital gains flow through the asset account. This implies that the marginal propensity to consume from dividend income is about the same as the marginal propensity to consume from total income, which in turn exceeds the marginal propensity to consume from capital gains.

Baker et al. (2007a) estimate that the marginal propensity to consume from dividend income is 0.49, the same as the marginal propensity to consume out of total income, whereas the marginal propensity to consume from total current-year returns is close to zero.

4.2.1.2 Options and Structured Products

Shefrin and Statman (1993a) apply the framework developed in Shefrin and Statman (1984) to other aspects of portfolio design. The general issue Shefrin and Statman (1993a) address how psychological issues impact the design and marketing of financial products, especially structured products.

Shefrin and Statman (1984) focus on the use of option strategies, most notably covered call writing, which has been the most popular option strategy for individual investors. Although considerations from neoclassical finance there indicate little merit to covered call writing, the same cannot be said for behavioral finance. Shefrin and Statman (1993a) use prospect theory to emphasize the framing elements inherent in a covered call strategy, noting how writing a call option which is fully covered by a holding the underlying stock masks a loss on the option when the stock price increases. Moreover, by segregating the option premium received from other cash flows such as dividends received, hedonic editing allows the premium to be emphasized psychologically, thereby generating an additional psychological benefit.

The analysis in Shefrin and Statman (1993a) identifies conditions under which investors will find it attractive to use options in particular ways such as writing call options on stocks in their possession, using put options for protection on stocks they hold, and purchasing call options for speculative purposes. Because of hedonic editing, the premium to be paid when purchasing put options for protection is detracting, just as the premium received when writing call options is enhancing.

Evidence discussed in Lakonishok et al. (2007) updates some of the discussion in Shefrin and Statman (1993a). Lakonishok et al. (2007) document the relative frequency of different option trading strategies by different classes of investors. They find that a large percentage of call writing stems from covered call positions. Surprisingly, they also find that volatility trading, using techniques emphasized in finance textbooks such as straddle positions, only accounts for a small fraction of option trading volume. Interestingly, most individual investors do not use protective puts. However, some do tend to use call options for speculative purposes. During the dot-com bubble, many did so for growth stocks, but not value stocks. Moreover, empirical evidence indicates that individual investors do not follow rational exercise strategies, as many exercise options prematurely (Poteshman and Serbin, 2003).

The mental accounting treatment of covered call writing involves the construction of mental accounts using both a stock and a call option. This feature indicates that mental accounts can be more complex than simple position holders for single assets. In this regard, McConnell and Schwartz (1992) describe how individual investors use the interest, but not principal, from their money market accounts to fund the purchase of out-of-the-money call options. This strategy provides both downside protection and upside potential, in accordance with the features emphasized in behavioral portfolio theory. McConnell and Schwartz (1992) describe this investing pattern as the motivation for the development of the liquid yield option note (LYON), a particular financial product with complex option properties. A key takeaway from the discussion is that when cognitive limits can prevent investors from making use of multiple securities to form complex mental accounts, financial engineers might be able to create value by doing so for them, by creating financial products such as the LYON.

4.2.2 Theoretical Issues

A traditional model of dynamic portfolio choice involves an expected utility maximizing investor choosing, at each time t, consumption (c_t)

and securities ($x_t = x_{t,1} \cdots, x_{t,J}$) given initial wealth ($W$), a stochastic stream of labor income (L_t), and stochastic prices (q_t) (Merton, 1971; Foldes, 1978). The standard Euler condition for this problem involves the purchase of a marginal unit of security j at time t, and requires that the marginal benefit of this purchase be equal to the marginal cost. The marginal benefit is the expected marginal utility of consumption at time $t+1$ generated by the marginal investment in security j. The marginal cost is the foregone marginal utility of consumption at time t, as the increased expenditure on security j comes at the expense of less consumption at time t.

In the traditional model, the expected utility function has the form:

$$E\left[\sum_t \delta^t u(c_t)\right], \tag{4.2}$$

where δ is a subjective time preference discount factor, and the expectation is taken over a subjective probability measure (P) which an investor associates with the underlying stochastic process. The Euler condition has the following form:

$$q_{t,j}\frac{\partial u}{\partial c_t} = E\left[q_{t+1,j}\delta\frac{\partial u}{\partial c_{t+1}}\right]. \tag{4.3}$$

In this setting, the purpose of the portfolio is to manage the risk profile of the investor's consumption stream, based on initial wealth (W) and stochastic labor income (L). This means that the portfolio serves to hedge uncertain labor income so as to smooth consumption over time. Unless labor income is highly volatile, most trading activity would involve marginal adjustments to a diversified portfolio with the purpose of rebalancing or dealing with liquidity needs to finance consumption.

Consider a behavioral analog to the traditional framework, with a view to modeling issues such as the disposition effect, attention hypothesis, use of dividends to finance consumption, status quo bias, and preference for positive skewness. See Hoffmann et al. (2010).

Begin with a full maximization extension to Equation (4.3), which we subsequently develop into a version featuring quasi-maximization. Write the analog of expected utility as an objective function U. Let U have as its arguments consumption stream $c = [c_t]$, portfolio choices

$x = [x_t]$, changes in portfolio positions $y = [x_t - x_{t-1}]$, prices $q = [q_t]$, and probability beliefs (P). The arguments c, x, and y are random variables. The inclusion of x, y, and q as arguments allows for an investor's preferences to reflect not only consumption, but also the performance of his or her portfolio and the impact of gains and losses from trading.

In the neoclassical framework, investors with predictable streams of labor income make small but frequent adjustments to their portfolios, by weighting the costs of foregone marginal current consumption associated with a marginal security purchase against the expected marginal future consumption so generated. Notice that the criterion driving portfolio choice is consumption and savings.

In the corresponding behavioral framework, the consumption–savings feature is augmented by additional considerations. When a behavioral investor contemplates a marginal increase in his or her holdings $x_{t,j}$ of security j at time t, (s)he adds three additional components to the neoclassical calculus. Those components take the form of $\partial U/\partial x_{t,j}$, $\partial U/\partial y_{t,j}$, and $\partial U/\partial y_{t+1,j}$. The behavioral Euler condition is:

$$q_{t,j}\frac{\partial U}{\partial c_t} = \sum_{t+1}\left(q_{t+1,j}\frac{\partial U}{\partial c_{t+1}}\right) + \frac{\partial U}{\partial x_t} + \frac{\partial U}{\partial y_t} - \sum_{t+1}\frac{\partial U}{\partial y_{t+1}}. \tag{4.4}$$

The term $\sum_{t+1}(q_{t+1,j}\partial U/\partial c_{t+1})$ is the analog to $E(q_{t+1,j}\delta\partial u/\partial c_{t+1})$, with the summation $\sum_{t+1}$ over the support of outcomes at $t+1$. Note that because of probability weighting, the behavioral expression might not correspond to an expectation with respect to the investor's beliefs. The term $\partial U/\partial x_t$ captures the effects of marginal evaluation utility, meaning the psychological effect the investor experiences from the value of his portfolio at different points in time. Here an investor's sense of well-being at a given moment, apart from his consumption, is enhanced when his or her portfolio grows, and is diminished when it falls. The terms $\partial U/\partial y_t$ and $\partial U/\partial y_{t+1}$ capture realization utility (Barberis and Huang, 2008), meaning the impact of trading a position. The minus sign associated with the term $\sum_{t+1}\partial U/\partial y_{t+1}$ in Equation (4.4) reflects the fact that increasing x_t reduces $y_{t+1} = x_{t+1} - x_t$. In this respect, an investor who sells at a gain might experience positive realization utility, whereas an investor who sells at a loss might experience negative realization utility (Thaler and Johnson, 1990).

A behavioral investor who contemplates a marginal increase in his or her holdings of security j at time t views the benefits in terms of utility from additional consumption at $t + 1$, increased evaluation utility at $t + 1$, and possibly increased realization utility at t. The corresponding cost is measured as foregone utility of consumption at t. Notably, the behavioral terms are unsigned. Depending on circumstances and the investor's characteristics, the additional behavioral terms can either serve to augment or reduce the benefits of a higher $x_{t,j}$.

The behavioral extension to the neoclassical portfolio choice model can be structured to incorporate the behavioral phenomena mentioned above. The extension involves issues related to preferences as well as issues related to biased beliefs. As to preferences, mental accounting, evaluation utility, and realization utility stem from the dependence of U upon x and y. Reference points and aspiration levels for both consumption and portfolio values can be embedded in the specific form for U. Gains and losses enter through the dependence of U on y. A similar statement applies to the disposition effect, with realization utility associated with gains or losses on a security, relative to a pre-specified reference point being a prime driver of whether or not to sell a security in the portfolio (Shefrin and Statman, 1985).

Status quo bias leads investors' reluctance to trade resulting, for example, from regret avoidance Samuelson and Zeckhauser (1988).[3] Benartzi and Thaler (2007) and Benartzi et al. (2009) document the strength of status quo bias in saving behavior. Mitchell et al. (2006) report that 80 percent of participants in 401(k) accounts initiate no trades in a two-year period, and an additional 11 percent make only one trade. Status quo bias significantly contributes to investors' lack of diversification. In our behavioral Euler condition (Equation (4.4))

[3] Regret is one component of realization utility, and relates to the consequence stemming from a reference action. The behavioral approach stresses the importance of reference points and aspiration levels. Notably, these might be based on perceived performance by others in an investor's peer group. A new line of inquiry investigates the role of social networks on investors' decisions (Kaustia and Knüpfer, 2009).

status quo bias is captured by $\partial U/\partial y_t < 0$ for $y_t > 0$ and $\partial U/\partial y_t > 0$ for $y_t < 0$ with a point of non-differentiability (kink) at $y_t = 0$.

Status quo bias does not mean that investors refrain from trading altogether, only that other forces must be strong enough to overcome their reluctance. Certainly, if the needs for hedging, rebalancing, and liquidity are sufficiently strong, investors will overcome status quo bias and trade. Likewise, investors can overcome status quo bias if they have enough conviction in their stock picking skills to feel little potential for regret (Kahneman et al., 1991) or derive sufficiently high evaluation utility from their portfolios.

In this last regard, Huddart et al. (2009) report that volume tends to spike when the price of a stock crosses a previous low or high. Moreover, the longer the time since the previous low or high, the larger the increase in volume. The effect is accentuated during periods when sentiment is high, as measured by Baker and Wurgler (2007), and is more concentrated in smaller stocks that are difficult to value, thereby suggesting that beliefs lie at the root of the issue. See also Statman et al. (2006) who document that trading volume is higher in rising markets than declining markets.

In the framework being sketched here, belief effects such as biases and ambiguity are encapsulated within the criterion function U. An example of a bias is overconfidence, which can lead investors to underestimate risk. Barber and Odean (2000) emphasize that overconfidence leads investors to trade too much, just the opposite of status quo bias. In one sense, the juxtaposition between the two effects highlights the nature of heterogeneity within the population. In another sense, the two coexist, in that active traders tend to concentrate their trades in just a few stocks.

Most individual investors have only the vaguest notion of how security returns are jointly distributed (Benartzi, 2001). For this reason, investors are unlikely to maximize fully. Instead, they are prone to engage in mental accounting, both to simplify the decision task and to exert self-control. Mental accounting is a key reason underlying the violation of stochastic dominance in the prospect theoretic choice experiments reported in Kahneman and Tversky (1979). This violation underscores the fact that prospect theory is not a framework for full maximization, but a heuristic-based framework to explain how people structure decision tasks and engage in quasi-optimization. In this regard, choice in prospect theory features an evaluation function which mimics the structure of an expected utility function, albeit imperfectly.

With this perspective in mind, I note that the beliefs used in connection with Equation (4.4) across securities might not be compatible with a single set of beliefs. Instead investors might apply Equation (4.4) on a security by security basis, or perhaps a mental account by mental account basis. As a result, the process for portfolio selection will resemble the process for consumer choice, with diversification corresponding to a "taste for variety." Moreover, quasi-maximization is likely to be accomplished in the context of a set of specific heuristics, as in Shefrin and Thaler (1988), which provides the formal BLC framework underlying the explanation for dividends advanced in Shefrin and Statman (1984). Behavioral portfolio models are also likely to feature a mixture of diffusion processes and jump processes, with portfolio composition changes reflecting jumps, as status quo bias is overcome.

5

Behavioralizing Asset Pricing Theory

Modern neoclassical asset pricing theory is built around the concept of a stochastic discount factor (SDF) (Cochrane, 2005; Foldes, 2000). The concept is very powerful, and allows most asset pricing models to be expressed as special cases of a general framework. The neoclassical SDF is structured as a monotone decreasing function, often interpreted as the marginal rate of substitution for a representative investor. In log–log space, the negative of the slope of the SDF is often interpreted as the representative investor's coefficient of relative risk aversion.

In many neoclassical models, the SDF is treated as time invariant. However, some authors use models displaying time variation in the SDF. Examples are Constantinides (1990) and Campbell and Cochrane (1999) which feature stochastic risk aversion, the result of habit formation. Habit formation involves the notion of reference consumption levels, and is therefore related to reference point-based behavioral preference models. As was mentioned in Sections 2 and 3, Kamstra et al. (2009) develops a model in which time varying, but deterministic, risk aversion reflects the medical condition "seasonal affective disorder" (SAD). SAD involves the impact of number of hours of sunlight on rates of depression in the population. In their previous published work, the authors find that in both the Northern and Southern hemispheres, stock returns tend to rise in the autumn as the number of hours of daylight falls, and rise in the spring as the number of hours of daylight increases.

As it happens, empirical estimates of the SDF show it to be oscillating rather than being monotone decreasing (Aït-Sahalia and Lo, 2000; Rosenberg and Engle, 2004). In this section I discuss how behavioral elements explain the oscillating shape. This section describes how the neoclassical SDF framework can be extended to capture behavioral beliefs and preferences, thereby behavioralizing asset pricing theory. The extension serves to identify both strengths and weaknesses in the behavioral approach. Much of the discussion below involves strengths. An example of a weakness involves market models in which investor preferences conform to prospect theory. De Giorgi et al. (2009) demonstrate that under plausible conditions, equilibrium will feature investors either holding (i) a risk-free portfolio or (ii) an unbounded portfolio.

As noted in Section 2, the behavioral asset pricing literature has mostly developed around two-asset models where the two assets are the risk-free security and a risky security. This statement applies to models designed to analyze the cross-section, which is clearly problematic, given that the cross-section features a multitude of securities.

The discussion below provides a formal definition for the SDF, briefly outlines the nature of a neoclassical SDF, describes the behavioral extension, and analyzes the implications of a behavioral SDF for particular asset classes.[1]

5.1 Stochastic Discount Factor

Consider the fundamental SDF-based asset pricing equation that the price q of an asset with random payoff x is the expected value of its discounted payoff, where m is the discount factor used to capture the effects of both time value of money and risk. Formally,

$$q = E[mx]. \tag{5.1}$$

[1] The first part of this section is drawn from Shefrin (2008c).

In Equation (5.1), both m and x are random variables. That is, the discount factor m typically varies across payoff levels in order to reflect that risk is priced differently across payoff levels.[2]

The SDF is a powerful concept, in that absent pure arbitrage opportunities, it underlies prices, returns, and risk premia associated with all assets, be they fixed income securities, equities, options, and other derivatives.

5.1.1 Neoclassical SDF

Think of the SDF m as state price per unit probability. In the neoclassical framework, m takes on higher values in unfavorable states than favorable states, giving rise to monotone declining shape across states.

The capital asset pricing model (CAPM) is an important special case of the SDF framework, and corresponds to the case when m is a linear function of the market return. Another special neoclassical case occurs when equilibrium prices are set as if there is a representative investor with correct beliefs and preferences that conform to constant relative risk aversion (CRRA). In this case, $log(m)$ is linear in the log of the gross market return.

As I mentioned above, in the neoclassical representative investor framework, m can be interpreted as a conditional marginal rate of substitution, the amount of current consumption the representative investor is willing to sacrifice in exchange for a marginal unit of future consumption in a particular state. In this regard, the negative slope of the neoclassical SDF reflects aversion to risk. The greater the degree of risk aversion, the steeper the slope. Risk neutrality corresponds to the case of a zero slope.

The SDF m also serves as a change of measure, transforming the true (also known as objective or physical) probability density function into the risk-neutral measure (Cochrane, 2005).

5.1.2 Behavioral SDF

Shefrin (2008a) establishes that when all investors have power utility, the log-SDF can be interpreted as the sum of a component relating

[2] Dividing by q leads to a similar expression on a return or per dollar basis, namely where R denotes the security return.

to fundamentals and a component relating to market sentiment. The market sentiment term Λ is the sum of a log-change of measure $ln(\xi)$ and a time preference shift term parameter δ_S.

$$\Lambda = ln(\xi) + ln(\delta_S). \tag{5.2}$$

The log-change of measure has the same interpretation as in Section 3, but for the probability density function associated with equilibrium prices rather than an individual investor. Just as in Section 3, bias is relative to probabilities associated with market efficiency. In this respect, prices of all securities are efficient when the corresponding log-change of measure is zero. Note that sentiment is a stochastic process whose underlying probabilities derive from the objective process for fundamentals. Sentiment reflects investors' misjudgments and misreactions to changing fundamentals, a result of suboptimal learning processes.

The fundamental variables entering the SDF are aggregate gross consumption growth g, a term γ measuring the market coefficient of relative risk aversion, and a term δ measuring the market time discount factor. The source of γ and δ is obtained from an aggregation procedure which is discussed below. Formally, the equation relating the log-SDF and sentiment has the form:

$$ln(m) = ln(\delta) - \gamma ln(g) + \Lambda. \tag{5.3}$$

Equation (5.3) indicates the manner in which sentiment impacts market prices through the SDF, especially its shape. In this regard, Equation (5.3) implies that when sentiment is zero, the log-SDF corresponds to the neoclassical case. However, if the magnitude of sentiment is sufficiently large, then Λ will drive the shape of the SDF. Figure 5.1 contrasts a neoclassical log-SDF and a behavioral log-SDF, both graphed against $ln(g)$. The neoclassical SDF is linear with a negative slope. The behavioral SDF depicted in the figure oscillates, with the probabilities of extreme negative events overweighted and extreme positive events underweighted. This type of SDF occurs when the market is dominated by a combination of overconfident optimists and underconfident pessimists, a case discussed in further detail below.

Using options data, Aït-Sahalia and Lo (2000) and Rosenberg and Engle (2004) estimate the empirical SDF, or more precisely its

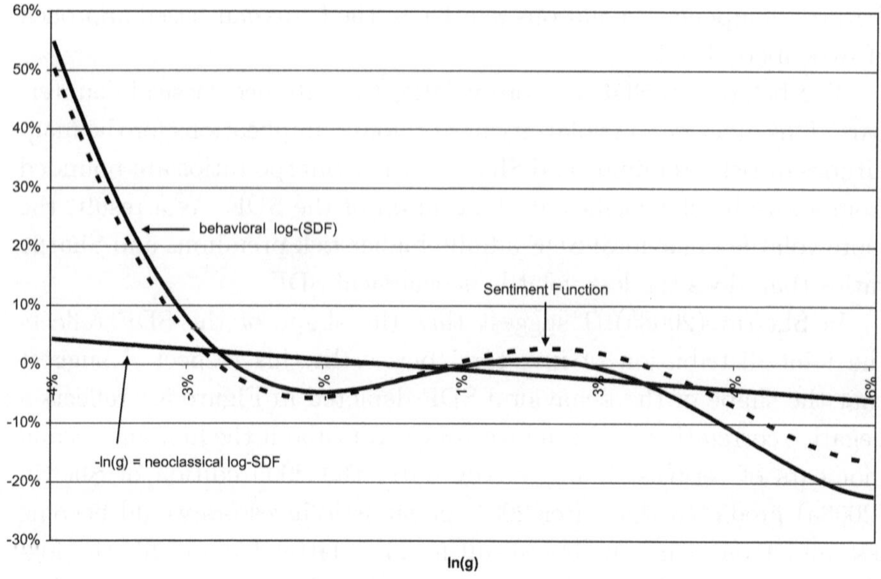

Fig. 5.1 Illustration of the decomposition in Equation (5.3), contrasting a behavioral SDF and a neoclassical SDF.

projection in respect to returns on the S&P 500. Both papers find that the empirical SDF has the behavioral shape portrayed in Figure 5.1.

The Rosenberg–Engle paper is especially interesting, in that the authors estimate the SDF in two ways. First, they restrict the SDF to have the traditional neoclassical shape displayed in Figure 5.1. Second, they use a free form Chebyshev polynomial procedure that involves no such restriction. This approach can be viewed as an inadvertent test of whether the empirical SDF is behavioral or not. Their empirical findings provide strong support that the SDF is behavioral.

Barone-Adesi et al. (2008) estimate the empirical SDF using a GARCH-based filtered historical simulation technique. Notably, their approach allows the objective pdf and risk-neutral pdf associated with the representative investor to feature different volatilities. In this regard, behavioral equilibrium naturally features differential volatilities for the objective pdf and risk-neutral pdf, largely because of the role played by sentiment Λ in the SDF m. The new GARCH-based filtered simulation approach produces a shape for the SDF which features dampened oscillations relative to the Gaussian-based approach of Rosenberg–Engle.

The behavioral SDF is more volatile than its neoclassical counterpart. This difference in volatility has profound implications for the magnitudes of risk premiums and Sharpe ratios. Sharpe ratios are bounded from above by the coefficient of variation of the SDF. As a result, the more volatile behavioral SDF admits higher risk premiums and Sharpe ratios than does the less volatile neoclassical SDF.

In Shefrin (2008a), I suggest that the shape of the SDF reflects the joint distribution of investors' biases. In this respect, I suggest that the shape of the behavioral SDF depicted in Figure 5.1 reflects a negative correlation between investors' errors about the first and second moments of returns. Using survey data, the 2005 edition of Shefrin (2008a) predicted that after 2001, pessimistic investors would become less underconfident, thereby resulting in a flatter left tail for the log-SDF depicted in Figure 5.1, see Figure 5.2. The findings reported in Barone-Adesi et al. (2008) indicate that the tail did indeed flatten in this period.

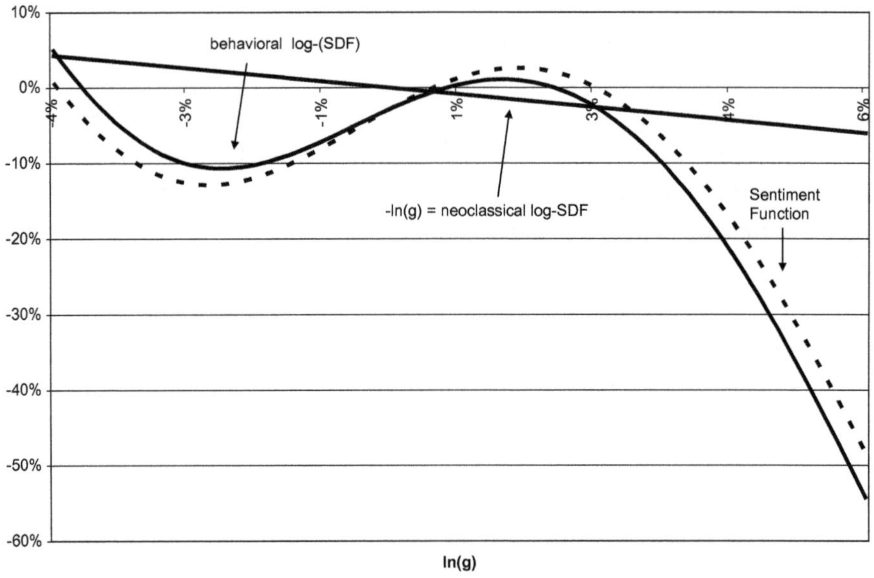

Fig. 5.2 Illustration of the impact of less underconfidence by pessimists in Figure 5.1.

5.2 How Markets Aggregate Investor Attributes

The empirical evidence strongly indicates that there is considerable heterogeneity in respect to investors' beliefs, degree of risk aversion, and rate of impatience. Some of this evidence is direct, meaning that it stems from surveys concerning these variables. Other evidence is indirect, being based on investors' decisions, such as the composition of their portfolios.[3] Therefore, a core issue in asset pricing theory is to understand how markets aggregate investors' beliefs and preferences. In regard to preferences, recall from the discussion in Section 3 that the change of measure technique applies both to preferences and to beliefs.

5.2.1 Aggregating Beliefs, Risk Tolerance, and Rates of Impatience

The study of the aggregation question dates back at least as far as Lintner (1969). Shefrin (2008a) presents an equilibrium aggregation result for a complete markets model featuring power utility. He demonstrates that the equilibrium market pdf is a generalized weighted Hölder average of the individual investors' pdfs, with the weights reflecting relative wealth or consumption, and the exponents being coefficients of relative risk aversion. Shefrin (2008a) also analyzes aggregation under the assumption of constant absolute risk aversion (CRRA), although he suggests that CARA is unrealistic from a behavioral perspective. Jouini and Napp (2006, 2007) establish similar results. They focus on the special case when investors share the same coefficient of relative risk aversion. Jouini and Napp's analysis of aggregation under the assumption of constant absolute risk aversion is more general.

For a detailed discussion of the aggregation theorems, readers are referred to Shefrin (2008a) and the works of Jouini and Napp (2007). For the purpose of the current discussion, it is sufficient to describe the general features of the representative investor for the case of power utility (CRRA). The log-SDF for the case when investors have

[3] In a series of papers, Barber et al. (2005), Barber et al. (2009a), and Barber et al. (2009b) provide evidence that individual investors as a group influence prices, but lose money to professional investors. However, they also document considerable heterogeneity, demonstrating that some individual investors possess superior skills.

CARA utility functions is similar in form, except that all averages are unweighted, rather than being consumption-weighted as is the case with CRRA utility (Shefrin, 2008a).

Heterogeneity leads the representative investor's beliefs to be different from those of the individual investors. For example, suppose that all investors have log-utility, share the same intertemporal discount factor δ, and have normally distributed beliefs with different means. In this case, the generalized weighted Hölder average is a simple wealth-weighted average of probability density functions. If the means are sufficiently different across investors, such a pdf can be multi-modal, and therefore non-normal. If investors differ in their intertemporal discount factors, the representative investor's stochastic process will typically violate Bayes' rule.

At any moment in time, the representative investor's degree of risk tolerance will be a consumption weighted convex combination of the individual investors' degree of risk tolerance. Because consumption shares are time varying, heterogeneity leads the representative investor's utility exponent γ to be state dependent. This means that γ will not measure the representative investor's degree of relative risk aversion.

The representative investor's intertemporal discount rate δ is a nonlinear function of the individual investors' discount rates. However, because the aggregation process relates to discount factors, not discount rates, the representative investor's discount factor will typically be non-exponential, even though every investor has an exponential discount factor. Moreover, because Hölder averages do not always sum to unity, the representative investor's discount rate will also reflect probability aggregation. Stated somewhat differently, the representative investor might exhibit aversion to ambiguity, even if none of the individual investors do.

The characteristics of the aggregation process hold clear lessons for asset pricing theorists of all stripes, neoclassical and behavioral. Typically, the market does not aggregate heterogeneous beliefs and preferences in a way that leads to the existence of a typical neoclassical representative investor, or a representative investor whose preferences and beliefs feature typical behavioral characteristics.

5.2.2 Liquidity Premium and Asymmetric Volatility

The preceding discussion describes the manner in which sentiment reflects the aggregation of investors' beliefs and preferences, while Equation (5.3) reflects the manner in which the SDF incorporates sentiment. In this respect, consider how market prices reflect a liquidity premium.

In Section 4, I made the point that liquidity issues can arise because at a given time t only a subset of investors actively trade. The others exhibit status quo bias which leads them to refrain from trading as a result of being situated at kinks in their preference maps. As a result, particular investors wishing to engage in trade at t might find that inducing sufficiently large positions on the part of their active trading partners requires market prices to move by a "nonnegligible" amount. In this respect, market prices at t, and hence sentiment, would reflect the beliefs and preferences of investors who engage in trade, but not investors who refrain from trade. It is in this sense that in the short-run sentiment reflects a liquidity premium.

As a general matter, the degree of status quo bias might be conditional on circumstances. For example, if regret potential increases after declines in aggregate consumption growth, then status quo bias might increase following declines in the return to the market portfolio. To the extent that the liquidity premium increases after such a decline, the result would be asymmetric volatility in the returns to particular securities. One indication of the extent to which status quo bias plays a role is the change in trading volume. Typically, an increase in status quo bias would lead to a decline in trading volume. In this regard, see Statman et al. (2006).

Asymmetric volatility might reflect asymmetric hot hand fallacy on the part of some investors, in the sense that investors predict stronger continuation after downturns than after upturns. At the same time, asymmetric hot hand fallacy would tend not to predict sharp upturns after steep declines, whereas status quo bias would.

5.2.3 Risk Aversion Puzzles

Assuming the existence of a typical neoclassical representative investor can lead to puzzles. For example, Jackwerth (2000) estimated the coefficient of absolute risk aversion for the market in the case when sentiment is (implicitly) zero. The papers by Aït-Sahalia and Lo (2000) and Rosenberg and Engle (2004) also estimate market risk aversion under the assumption that sentiment is zero. All of these studies find coefficients of risk aversion for the market that are extreme. Reasonable benchmark values for the coefficient of relative risk aversion (CRRA) involve the range 1.5–3.5, with a few outliers between 0 and 1 and between 5 and 6.5.

The Aït-Sahalia-Lo range for CRRA is 1–60. The Rosenberg–Engle estimated range for the CRRA is 2–12, with a mean of 7.6. Moreover, they find that market risk aversion is highly variable over time. Jackwerth (2000) estimates imply that the market's coefficient of CRRA ranges between −14 and 27. Negative values, which indicate risk seeking, are especially surprising. Blackburn and Ukhov (2006), which extends Jackwerth's analysis from the market to individual stocks, also features highly variable rates of risk aversion that take on exotic values.

However, negative values for CRRA and values over 6 are at odds with survey data. Jackwerth points out that the shape of the absolute risk aversion function, which he estimates for the market, is not monotone declining and time invariant, as neoclassical theory would suggest. Instead, it mostly tends to be U-shaped and time varying.

The culprit in these risk aversion estimation exercises is the assumption that sentiment is zero, with the SDF conforming to a monotone decreasing function. If sentiment is nonzero in practice, and oscillates, then the upward sloping segments will appear to imply negative risk aversion. Incorrectly assuming it to be zero in theory forces the models' risk aversion parameters to pick up the effects of market sentiment, such as optimism, pessimism, and overconfidence.

5.3 Aggregation and the Shape of Sentiment

The easiest way to understand the shape of sentiment is by working with examples featuring log-utility. Consider a complete market model featuring two investors, whose initial wealth levels are equal. Suppose that both investors have log-utility functions. Assume that the log of consumption growth is normally distributed, and that both investors believe it to be normally distributed. However, let the two investors disagree about the first moment. Assume that one investor is excessively bullish about mean consumption growth, while the second investor is excessively bearish about mean consumption growth. For now, let both investors hold correct beliefs about the second moment. Notably, in the special case of log-utility, the Hölder average becomes a simple convex combination.

As pointed out in Section 3, associated with the bullish investor is a log-change of measure which is linear with positive slope. Associated with the bearish investor is a log-change of measure which is linear with negative slope. Recall that the market equilibrium aggregates pdfs, not log-change of measure functions. The resulting log-change of measure for the representative investor will be U-shaped. Therefore, the bearish investor drives the shape of market sentiment for unfavorable states, whereas the bullish investor drives the shape of market sentiment for favorable states. Notably, a U-shape implies that the market overweights the probabilities of extreme events, be they favorable or unfavorable.

If investors are overconfident, then they will underestimate the probabilities of extreme events. As a result, the sentiment function can have an inverse U-shape. The inverse-U can be interpreted as reflecting the "black swan effect:" (Taleb, 2007). See Odean (1998b) for the first theoretical treatment dedicated to the question of how overconfidence impacts asset prices.

Finally, if bearish investors tend to be underconfident, in that they overpredict the probabilities of crashes, while bullish investors tend to be overconfident, then the sentiment function will tend to be oscillating, as depicted in Figure 5.1.

5.4 Risk and Return

5.4.1 Behavioral Mean-Variance Returns

A mean-variance (MV) portfolio is a portfolio of assets that maximizes expected return for a specified return variance. In neoclassical asset pricing, where sentiment is zero, the risk premium for a security is based on its return covariance with any risky mean-variance portfolio. For example, in the CAPM the market portfolio is mean-variance efficient, and this is why risk premiums are based on the covariance between the security's returns and the returns to the market portfolio. In the case of CAPM, the SDF is linear and negatively sloped.

How does sentiment impact the relationship between risk and return? The short answer is in the same way as in neoclassical asset pricing. Because risk premiums for all securities are based on return covariance with MV portfolios, even when sentiment is nonzero, the key lies in understanding how sentiment impacts the nature of the return distributions for both MV portfolios and individual assets. This means appreciating that systematic risk, meaning risk which is priced, has both a fundamental component and a sentiment component.

The SDF can be used to price all assets, including portfolios. Hence, the SDF also prices all mean-variance efficient portfolios, and therefore the SDF can be used to generate the return distribution for an MV portfolio. Just as in neoclassical asset pricing theory, the SDF generates the mean-variance frontier. The relationship is the same. Effectively, the return to a risky mean-variance porfolio is a linear function of the SDF, with a negative slope coefficient. Therefore, the shape of a mean-variance portfolio return function is obtained by inverting and tilting the SDF (Cochrane, 2005; Shefrin, 2005).

Figure 5.3 contrasts the return pattern for a behavioral mean-variance portfolio to the return pattern for a neoclassical mean-variance portfolio. Each curve in Figure 5.3 is a plot of the linear function described in Shefrin (2008a) that links the return of an MV portfolio to the consumption growth rate through the SDF. The behavioral MV curve corresponds to the case in which sentiment is given by Figure 5.1, whereas the neoclassical MV curve corresponds to the case when sentiment is zero. Notice that the shapes in Figure 5.3 correspond to the inverted, tilted shapes in Figure 5.1.

Figure 5.3 has three points worthy of note. First, the return to a traditional MV portfolio is approximately the return to a portfolio consisting of the market portfolio and the risk-free security. For the purpose of illustration, the weight attached to the risk-free asset in both portfolios is high.

Second, the return to a behavioral MV portfolio is more volatile than the return to a traditional MV portfolio. This is because the peaks and

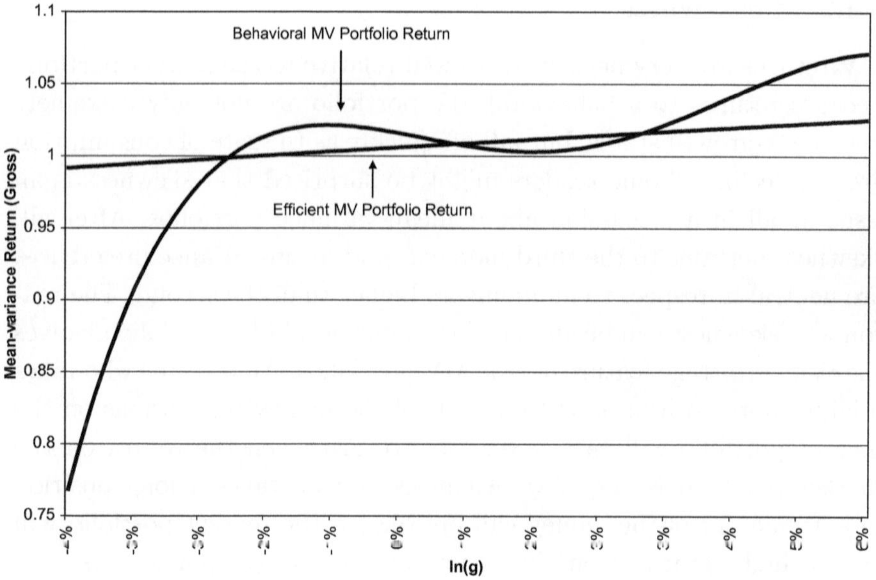

Fig. 5.3 This figure contrasts the return pattern for a neoclassical MV portfolio and a behavioral MV portfolio associated with Figure 5.1.

valleys in the behavioral MV portfolio correspond to exposure from risky arbitrage. This is a true MV portfolio, based on the objective pdf. Therefore, maximizing expected return involves the exploitation of nonzero sentiment.

Notice that in Figure 5.1, sentiment is positive at the extreme left and negative at the extreme right. This means that extreme out-of-the-money put options on the market portfolio are overpriced, while extreme out-of-the-money call options are underpriced. As a result, a true mean-variance portfolio would feature a short position in extreme out-of-the-money put options on the market portfolio and a long position in extreme out-of-the-money call options on the market portfolio.

Third, expected returns and risk premiums for securities are determined by security betas, taken with respect to a risky mean-variance portfolio benchmark. In this case the risk premium to a security is the product of the security's beta and the risk premium of the mean-variance benchmark.

5.4.2 Coskewness

MV-returns are very negatively skewed relative to the market portfolio because returns to a behavioral MV-portfolio are not only extremely low in low-growth states, but fall off quickly as the rate of consumption growth declines. Some readers might be surprised that skewness is an issue at all in a discussion about mean-variance portfolios. After all, skewness pertains to the third moment, and mean-variance preferences are neutral in respect to all moments higher than the second. The reason why skewness can be an issue for a behavioral MV portfolio involves the risky arbitrage feature of true MV portfolios. An investor who takes a large short position in extreme out-of-the-money put options on the market portfolio will earn a very low return when the return on the market portfolio is very low. An investor who takes a long position in extreme out-of-the-money call options on the market portfolio will earn a high return when the return on the market portfolio is very high.

To understand the implications that the behavioral MV shape in Figure 5.3 has for the nature of risk premiums for individual securities, consider what systematic risk entails. Systematic risk is risk associated with the returns to an MV portfolio. Securities whose returns are highly correlated with the returns to an MV portfolio will be associated with high degrees of systematic risk. In this regard, remember that the returns to the behavioral MV portfolio depicted in Figure 5.3 are negatively skewed relative to the market portfolio. Therefore, securities whose returns are high in systematic risk will feature negative skewness relative to the market portfolio.

Following Barone-Adesi and Talwar (1983), Harvey and Siddique (2000) study the cross-section of stock returns using coskewness relative to the market portfolio. They propose several definitions of coskewness. One definition of coskewness is the beta of the security's return relative to the squared market return, controlling for covariation with the market return. With this definition, coskewness measures the extent to which a security's return covaries with the squared market return.

The definition of coskewness is particularly appropriate when the SDF has a quadratic-like U-shape. Recall that the SDF will be

U-shaped when the sentiment component has a U-shape and is large relative to the fundamental component of the SDF. In this case, the shape of the MV function is an inverted-U. Observe that this type of MV return function will feature negative coskewness with respect to the market portfolio. In this situation, a security that is high in systematic risk, meaning risk that is priced, will mimic the MV-return pattern, and therefore also feature negative coskewness. This is because coskewness measures the amount of mean-variance skewness that a security's return adds to an investor's portfolio. Coskewness plays a role analogous to a factor loading in a multifactor asset pricing model. Notably, there is a negative premium to holding stocks whose returns exhibit positive coskewness relative to the market portfolio.

Of course, the shape of the behavioral MV return pattern depicted in Figure 5.3 is not exactly an inverted-U. In the right portion of Figure 5.3, the behavioral MV-return pattern does not have the same feature as an inverted-U. However, in the left portion, the patterns are similar. This suggests that when sentiment has the shape depicted in Figure 5.1, negative coskewness with respect to the market portfolio will capture some, but not all, aspects of systematic risk. See Barone-Adesi et al. (2004) for evidence that this is the case.

Harvey and Siddique (2000) study coskewness using a four-factor model, where the factors are, respectively, the market return, size, book-to-market equity, and momentum. Harvey and Siddique find that the correlation between coskewness and mean returns of portfolios sorted by size, book-to-market equity, and momentum is -0.71. This means that much of the explanatory power of size, book-to-market equity (B/M), and momentum in the returns of individual stocks plausibly derives from coskewness.

Harvey and Siddique point out that the market factor by itself explains only 3.5 percent of cross-sectional returns. However, the combination of the market factor and coskewness explains 68.1 percent of cross-sectional returns. This value rivals the 71.8 percent associated with the use of the market factor, size, and B/M. For momentum, recent winners feature lower coskewness than that of recent losers. All of these findings are consistent with MV portfolio returns having the shape depicted in Figure 5.3.

Dittmar (2002) discusses the superiority of nonlinear models over linear factor models such as the Fama–French three-factor model. He develops a flexible nonlinear pricing kernel approach which is in the tradition of a zero sentiment representative investor model. Notably, he finds that the empirical SDF in his analysis is not monotone decreasing over its range, but instead has a U-shaped pattern. In this regard, Poti (2006) uses a quadratic U-shaped SDF to extend the Harvey–Siddique analysis.

5.4.3 Decomposition of Risk Premiums

Let Z be an arbitrary security with return r_Z. Letting $\Phi = exp(\Lambda)$ define

$$h_Z = \frac{E[\delta \Phi g^{-\gamma} r_Z]}{E[\delta g^{-\gamma} r_Z]}, \tag{5.4}$$

where the expectation is taken with respect to the true underlying stochastic process Π. Keeping in mind that Φ is proportional to a change of measure, the impact of the numerator of Equation (5.4) is to shift probability weight across different realizations of the product $g^{-\gamma} r_Z$. Suppose that we shift probability to higher valued realizations, and take the expectation with respect to the true underlying process. In this case $h_Z > 1$, and so the third term on the right-hand side of Equation (5.5) is negative. Relative to fundamental value $E[\delta g^{-\gamma} r_Z]$, h_Z represents the degree to which Z is overpriced (when $h_Z > 1$) and underpriced (when $h_Z < 1$).

Shefrin (2008a) establishes that the risk premium associated with Z is given by:

$$E[r_Z] - i_1 = (i_{1,e} - i_1) - \frac{Cov[g^{-\gamma} r_Z]}{E[g^{-\gamma}]} + i_{1,e} \frac{1 - h_Z}{h_Z}, \tag{5.5}$$

where i_1 is the market risk-free rate of interest, and $i_{1,e}$ is the value of the risk-free rate when sentiment is zero and prices are efficient. When prices are efficient, $i_1 = i_{1,e}$. Notice that when investor errors lead to an increase in the risk-free rate, the risk premium on Z declines.

Equation (5.5) has a straightforward interpretation. When sentiment Λ is zero, then Equation (5.4) implies that $h_Z = 1$. In this case, the third term on the right-hand side of Equation (5.5) is zero. In addition, $i_{1,e} - i_1 = 0$ so that when prices are efficient, Equation (5.5) is just equal to the middle term on the right-hand side. When sentiment Λ is nonzero, Equation (5.4) implies that h_Z may not be equal to 1. Notice that Z being overpriced causes its risk premium to decline relative to the case of market efficiency.[4]

Observe that the expression (5.5) for the risk premium decomposes into a fundamental component (the middle term on the right-hand side) and a sentiment component (the first and third terms). In this respect, when prices are inefficient, the first and third terms are typically nonzero. The variable h_Z measures the degree to which security Z is overpriced. For example, if $h_Z = 2$, then Z is overpriced by 100 percent. Equation (5.5) indicates that the overvaluation of Z causes the expected return to Z to change by $\frac{i_{1,e}(1-h_Z)}{h_Z}$ which in this case equals 50 percent$(= \frac{1-2}{2})$ of what the gross risk free rate would be were prices efficient.

5.4.3.1 Cross-Section

Equation (5.5) specifies how the cross-section is driven by a combination of fundamental risk and sentiment-based risk.[5] Fundamental risk is determined by the return covariance with the fundamental component of the SDF. Conditional on the interest rate, sentiment risk is determined by the term $\frac{1-h_Z}{h_Z}$.[6]

In addition to the discussion about coskewness, and its connection to the cross-section, I also want to mention some experimental evidence. For the last decade, I have surveyed money managers, analysts,

[4] This statement is conditional on the equilibrium return distribution r_Z. Notably, the equilibrium return distribution to Z might be different in the case when prices are inefficient relative to the case when they are efficient. Think about an out-of-the-money call option in an example when the representative investor is excessively optimistic. The excessive optimism will increase the price of the option, thereby left shifting and distorting its objective return distribution at a given node in the uncertainty tree.

[5] Equation (5.5) should be understood with reference to the projection of sentiment onto the returns for individual securities.

[6] In Section 4 I mentioned that the framework for behavioral portfolio selection resembles the framework for consumer choice, as some investors build portfolios with only a vague understanding of covariance. This feature does not negate Equation (5.5), as long as some investors are able to exploit, and eliminate, pure arbitrage opportunities.

and students to elicit their judgments about risk and return in connection with the cross-section. The general finding from this survey is that although those surveyed believe that in theory risk and return are positively related, in practice they form judgments as if the two are negatively related.

Judgments about risk are consistent with the neoclassical framework. Most of those surveyed judge that risk is positively related to market beta, book-to-market equity, and recent momentum, while negatively related to market capitalization. In contrast to the neoclassical framework, most also believe that the relationship between expected returns and these same variables has the opposite sign as with risk. Not surprisingly, judgments about risk and return turn out to be negatively related.

Two psychological principles might be at work in explaining why people form judgments as if they believe that risk and return are negatively related. The first is representativeness. People might rely on a heuristic whereby they believe that the stocks of good companies are representative of good stocks. The second is that both low risk and high returns generate positive affect, and so the affect heuristic can also explain the negative relationship.

Baker and Wurgler (2006, 2007) discuss various measures of sentiment that have been used in behavioral studies. They then develop a new index of sentiment based on the following six specific measures:

— closed-end fund discount,
— detrended log-turnover,
— number of IPO,
— first-day return on IPOs,
— dividend premium, and
— equity share in new issues.

Baker and Wurgler suggest that sentiment will impact prices of some stocks more than others. They suggest that the returns to stocks which are difficult both to value and to arbitrage will be more sensitive to sentiment than stocks which are both easier to value and easier to arbitrage. The heart of their argument involves the concept of a sentiment seesaw. When sentiment is high, speculative difficult-to-arbitrage stocks become overvalued, and safe easy-to-arbitrage stocks become undervalued. When sentiment is low, the reverse occurs. A notable feature of the analysis is that because of mispricing, stocks that appear to be riskier in terms of fundamentals, can feature lower expected returns than safer stocks.

In Baker–Wurgler, a stock's sensitivity to sentiment is measured in terms of a sentiment beta. A sentiment beta explains the sentiment component of the risk premium. Conditional on the risk-free rate, this component effectively corresponds to the third term in the right-hand side of Equation (5.5); unconditionally, it corresponds to the sum of the first and third terms.

Empirically, Baker–Wurgler report that returns are predictable, conditional on the value of sentiment in the prior month. When past sentiment has been high, subsequent returns to speculative stocks, more difficult-to-arbitrage stocks are indeed lower than returns to safer stocks which are easier to arbitrage. Conversely, when past sentiment has been low, subsequent returns to speculative stocks, more difficult-to-arbitrage stocks are higher than to safer stocks which are easier to arbitrage.

5.5 Long-run Fitness

The neoclassical perspective has tended to be that information investors will exploit any inefficiencies immediately, so that prices are efficient at all times. In contrast, the behavioral position is different, namely that in the short-run, limits to arbitrage can prevent market prices from being efficient. The conditions for efficiency essentially require that the average investor error be zero, so that investor bias is unsystematic, and that the covariance between investor error and investor wealth be zero, so that any errors are not concentrated within the investor population (Shefrin and Statman, 1994). In contrast to the neoclassical perspective, the behavioral perspective holds that information traders, meaning investors who are free from error, will not guarantee market efficiency, because information investors are typically reluctant to take on the risk associated with the large positions required to eliminate inefficiencies completely.

What about the long-run? Will the existence of information traders eliminate any price inefficiencies? The neoclassical answer to this question is yes, with the argument being that investors who are subject to error will lose their wealth to information investors. In contrast, the behavioral answer has been not necessarily, that investors who are subject to error can take on more risk than information investors, thereby earning higher returns in the long-run, and surviving.

Lawrence Summers first proposed the intuition underlying the behavioral perspective, and the idea was formally discussed by DeLong et al. (1991). Their framework features CRRA utility functions, and describes conditions under which investors who are prone to error survive in the long-run and impact prices.

The analysis in DeLong et al. (1991) is controversial. In particular, the main result is at odds with the general literature on long-term survivability or fitness. This literature has recently been surveyed by Blume and Easley (2008). At the center of the fitness lies the concept of entropy. Given two discrete probability density functions Π and P over a series of K states, define

$$I_{\Pi}(P) = \sum_{k=1}^{K} \Pi(k) ln(\Pi(k)/P(k)), \tag{5.6}$$

and call this variable the relative entropy of P with respect to Π.

Consider a set of investors indexed by j. Suppose that objective probabilities correspond to Π. Blume and Easley establish that the time average of investor j's marginal utility to investor k's marginal utility is given by:

$$[ln(\delta_k) - I_{\Pi}(P_k)] - [(ln(\delta_j) - I_{\Pi}(P_j)]. \tag{5.7}$$

They call the difference $[ln(\delta_j) - I_{\Pi}(P_j)]$ investor j's *survival index.* Suppose that investor j has a lower survival index than investor k. Then with probability one, the ratio of investor j's marginal utility approaches $+\infty$. However, if physical resources are bounded from above and investor utility is CRRA with risk aversion parameter $\gamma_j \geq 1$, then over time investor j's consumption must go to zero.

Notice that there are two components to the survival index. The first component relates to patience, and the second to errors in beliefs. The survival condition suggests that long-run fitness is determined by being sufficiently patient relative to other investors and/or being sufficiently better informed about objective probabilities.

Setting aside impatience, the results in Blume and Easley (2008) indicate that informed investors will dominate pricing in the long-run. This means that there is good reason to believe that the fundamental assertion put forth in DeLong et al. (1991) is incorrect. Indeed, Blume and Easley (2008) state that they have difficulty following the logic in the latter paper. In this respect, the model appears to be vaguely specified, with the formal argument being loose.

Of course, it is entirely possible that investors with erroneous beliefs persist in the long run, but for reasons different from those suggested in the analysis of DeLong et al. (1991). For example, there may be no informed investors at all, in that all investors are subject to some form of error or bias. Alternatively, the market can feature incompleteness in combination with overlapping generations with finite lifetimes. Therefore, better informed investors might not live long enough to extract most of the wealth from their less informed counterparts. Moreover, even if they did so, their heirs might not possess the same degree of superiority.

5.6 Pricing Dynamics

A stream of literature is developing that focuses on asset pricing dynamics. The volume edited by Hens and Schenk-Hoppé (2008) contains many interesting contributions, not the least being the survey by Blume and Easley mentioned above. Dumas et al. (2009) build on the work of Scheinkman and Xiong (2003), who assume that the aggregate consumption growth rate follows a mean-reverting diffusion process with a time varying stochastic drift. Investors do not observe the drift directly. Instead they receive a noisy signal whose change is equal to the sum of drift plus a noise term that is uncorrelated with the change in drift. All investors make forecasts of the change in drift. However, some investors overreact to their forecast errors for the rate of change in the signal. In this respect, they read more into their signal forecast errors than is appropriate, because they believe that the noisy signal features a positive correlation with the change in drift. As a result, they overweight the contribution of their signal forecast errors when predicting how the drift term will subsequently change. This overweighting leads them to underestimate drift volatility, thereby leading to overconfidence on their part.

The term structure of interest rates provides fertile ground for applying behavioral asset pricing models. From a neoclassical perspective, interest rate spreads and movements pose major puzzles. Two prominent examples are the expectations hypothesis and the credit spread puzzle for corporate debt. The expectations hypothesis requires that the expected risk adjusted return to a long default-free bonds should be equal to the expected return from rolling over short-term risk-free bonds over the life of the long bond. Realized bond yield volatility exceeds the upper bound limit implied by the expectations hypothesis (Shiller, 1978). The credit spread puzzle relates to the fact that the common factors explaining default probabilities explain at most 25 percent of the variation in spreads. Moreover, there appears to be a common latent factor which explains 75 percent of the residual. Bond yields are more sensitive to macroeconomic announcements (Gurkaynak et al., 2005; Duffie et al., 2007). In this regard, Equation (5.5) comes to mind, both as a factor in explaining the failure of the expectations hypothesis and the existence of the credit spread puzzle.

5.6.1 Behavioral Interest Rate Models

In a general SDF-based framework, Equation (5.1) stipulates that the price of any security is given by $q = E[mx]$. For zero coupon risk-free bonds, x can be taken to be 1, and so bond prices are simply given by $E[m]$, where the expectation is taken with respect to objective probabilities. Of course, for risky bonds, $x \neq 1$.

Equivalently, in a CRRA-framework the price of zero coupon risk-free bonds can be expressed as $q = E[\delta(t)g^{-\gamma}]$, where the expectation is taken with respect to the representative investor's pdf (Shefrin, 2008a). With $g^{-\gamma}$ being a convex function, $E[g^{-\gamma}] \geq E[g]^{-\gamma}$. Beginning with the case of certainty, in which case $E[g^{-\gamma}] = E[g]^{-\gamma}$. Notice that applying a mean preserving spread will increase the bond price, thereby lowering the associated interest rate.

A clue to why the expectations hypothesis fails comes from understanding that bond prices are determined by the representative investor's pdf in $q = E[\delta(t)g^{-\gamma}]$, rather than the objective pdf. At the margin, the representative investor is quite willing to substitute a roll-over strategy involving short-bonds for a long-bond. However, if sentiment is nonzero, then this substitution would be ill advised for a representative investor with correct beliefs. In other words, the expectations hypothesis might hold subjectively, relative to the beliefs that underlie equilibrium prices, but not objectively, where it is the objective probabilities that underlie the dynamics of bond returns and yields.

One thing that distinguishes a behavioral theory of bond pricing from a neoclassical theory is the nature of the SDF. A neoclassical SDF is monotone decreasing and stable over time, whereas a behavioral SDF oscillates and is prone to being volatile over time. In a behavioral approach, Equation (5.5) captures how nonzero sentiment leads bond returns to feature both fundamental and sentiment-based components.

Consider an example of a behavioral term structure theory as developed in Shefrin (2008a). The example features log-utility investors with heterogeneous beliefs. As was mentioned above, the equilibrium market pdf is a generalized weighted Hölder average of the individual investors' pdfs, with the weights reflecting relative wealth or consumption, and the exponents being coefficients of relative risk aversion. In the special case of log-utility, the Hölder average is a simple convex combination. As a result, the SDF will also have the form of a convex combination. This is very convenient, as it leads market prices to be expressed as convex combinations of prices that would occur in a series of hypothetical homogeneous belief models. In particular, bond prices will be convex combinations of bond prices that would occur in a series of homogeneous belief examples.

The preceding section about aggregation and the shape of sentiment discusses an example with just two investors, one bullish and the other bearish. In this two-investor example, homogeneous beliefs which are independent and identically distributed (i.i.d.) lead the yield curve to be flat. However, heterogeneous beliefs lead the yield curve to be downward sloping, a consequence of yield being a convex function of bond price. In the homogeneous case, bond prices decline with maturity to preserve constant yield. Notably, the decline is larger for the higher yield. Therefore, as the maturity increases, consider what happens to the ratio of the bond price for the investor associated with lower yield to the bond price for the investor associated with the higher yield. This ratio grows with maturity. Hence, the wealth weighted average convex combination of bond prices at different maturities will lead to the lower yield being emphasized. The result will be a declining yield curve.

5.6.1.1 Modeling Interest Rate Dynamics

Consider how the style of models developed in Scheinkman and Xiong (2003) and Dumas et al. (2009) provide insight into the dynamics of interest rates. In a promising approach, Xiong and Yan (2009) extend the log-utility example from Shefrin (2008a) from a discrete exchange economy to a continuous production economy. Just as Shefrin (2008a) suggests that the two investor log-utility heterogeneity model can capture the oscillating shape displayed by the empirical SDF, Xiong and Yan (2009) suggest that a two-investor log-utility model can capture important features of interest rate dynamics. Notably, they confirm the failure of the expectations hypothesis. They also confirm the tendency for wealth fluctuations to amplify volatility and time variation in bond prices and premia. Most importantly, they offer an explanation for a tent-shaped linear combination of forward rates to explain bond return dynamics.

At the heart of the dynamics in Xiong and Yan (2009) are a set of assumptions about consumption growth and investment. The returns to investment dI_t/I_t follow a diffusion process with instantaneous drift f_t, Brownian motion $Z_I(t)$, and standard deviation σ_I. The equation governing dI_t/I_t is:

$$\frac{dI_t}{I_t} = f_t dt + \sigma_I dZ_I(t). \tag{5.8}$$

Because Equation (5.8) is a linear production process relating to the instantaneous marginal rate of transformation between current and future consumption, Xiong and Yan (2009) show that it effectively determines the instantaneous risk-free rate of interest $r_t = f_t - \sigma_I^2$.

However, f_t itself is determined by a mean reverting diffusion process with a tendency to revert to an unobservable long-run mean l_t according to:

$$df_t = -\lambda f(f_t - l_t)dt + \sigma_f dZ_f(t), \tag{5.9}$$

where λ_f governs the mean reverting speed of f_t. Finally, l_t follows an Ornstein–Uhlenbeck process:

$$dl_t = -\lambda_l(l_t - \bar{l})dt + \sigma_l dZ_l(t), \tag{5.10}$$

where λ_l governs the mean reverting speed of l_t. The variables in these equations that are not identified relate to the associated Brownian motions and their coefficients.

Together, Equations (5.8)–(5.10) imply:

$$dr_t = -\lambda_f(t)[r_t - (l_t - \sigma_f^2)]dt + \sigma_f dZ_f. \tag{5.11}$$

Equation (5.14) is common in the bond pricing literature (Balduzzi et al., 1998).

Equations (5.8)–(5.10) provide the basis for the objective processes governing the evolution of aggregate consumption growth. These are conditional on publicly available information at t represented by $\{f_\tau\}_{\tau=0}^t$, and determine a process for a conditional objective density for $\{l_t|\{f_\tau\}_{\tau=0}^t\}$. The two investors in Xiong and Yan (2009) hold biased beliefs. They observe a white noise signal $dS_t = dZ_S(t)$ which they mistakenly believe to be informative about the fundamental shock l_t. Moreover, the two investors' reactions to dS_t are equal and opposite, so that one investor acts bullishly and the other bearishly. Each investor's subjective estimate of l_t at t is conditioned on $\{f_\tau, S(\tau)\}_{\tau=0}^t$. Denote an estimate of l_t by $\hat{l}_t$.

Xiong and Yan (2009) establish that in equilibrium featuring homogeneity, the bond price at time t of a zero coupon default-free bond with maturity τ has the form:

$$B_H(\tau, f_t, \hat{l}_t) = e^{-a_f(\tau)f_t - a_l(\tau)\hat{l}_t - b(\tau)}. \tag{5.12}$$

The corresponding yield is given by:

$$Y_H(\tau, f_t, \hat{l}_t) = -\frac{1}{\tau}log(B^H). \tag{5.13}$$

In terms of yield, the loading factor on f_t has a value of 1 for maturity $\tau = 0$, which monotonically decreases to zero with maturity length. The loading factor on the estimate $\hat{l}_t$ turns out to be hump shaped, achieving a maximum impact at intermediate maturities, and plays a central role in the results of Xiong and Yan (2009). The yields of bonds with very long maturities have low exposure to $\hat{l}_t$, as l_t reverts to $\bar{l}$ in the long-run.

As in Shefrin (2008a), heterogeneous beliefs lead equilibrium bond prices in Xiong and Yan (2009) to be wealth-weighted convex combinations of bond prices in homogeneous belief economies. Wealth shifts from trading based on differential beliefs lead to excess volatility in bond prices, a feature emphasized in Shefrin and Statman (1994). The SDF in Xiong and Yan (2009) follows a process dm_t/m_t which decomposes into a fundamental component and a sentiment component. The fundamental component is $-r_t dt - \sigma_I dZ_I$. The sentiment component is proportional to the difference between the objective estimate $\hat{l}_t$ and the representative investor's estimate formed as a wealth-weighted convex combination of the individual investors' estimates. The stochastic term in the sentiment component is the Brownian motion $d\hat{Z}_f^R$ underlying the objective estimate $\hat{l}_t$.

The equation for dm_t/m_t indicates the percentage change in the SDF over the next interval of length dt. Because the instantaneous interest rate is given by the expected value of m, consumption growth fundamentals will lead the log-SDF to decline at rate r plus a random shock to aggregate consumption growth. Sentiment introduces a second shock, based on the magnitude of the error in the representative investor's estimate of l_t relative to the statistically optimal estimate. If the representative investor's estimate is too low and $d\hat{Z}_f^R > 0$, then the sentiment component will exert upward pressure on dm_t/m_t, thereby counteracting the tendency of state prices to fall with time.

An important contribution of Xiong and Yan (2009) is to analyze the relationship between bond maturity and return volatility. They show that in a homogeneous belief economy, the relationship is monotone decreasing. However, in a heterogeneous belief economy, the relationship is hump shaped, similar to the empirical results in Dai and Singleton (2003). Xiong and Yan (2009) explain that the reason for the different shape in the heterogeneous beliefs case, relative to the homogeneous beliefs case, lies with the factor weightings in Equations (5.12) and (5.13). Essentially, the weighting on the f_t factor dominates the weighting on the $\hat{l}_t$ in the homogeneous beliefs case, whereas wealth shift dynamics can induce sufficient volatility in $\hat{l}_t$ to inject the hump.

One way to think about the expectations hypothesis is through the following equation developed in Campbell and Shiller (1991).

$$Y_{t+1}(n-1) - Y_t(n) = \alpha_n + \beta_n \frac{Y_t(n) - Y_t(1)}{n-1}. \tag{5.14}$$

When the expectations hypothesis holds $\beta_n = 1$. This is because when $Y_t(n) - Y_t(1) > 0$, there will be an advantage to investing in the long-bond, unless its price falls sufficiently, thereby driving up its yield. However, the empirical evidence indicates that β_n is close to zero and positive for 2-month maturities and then declines to about -4 for 10-year maturities. Therefore, in practice, when the yield spread is positive, long-term yields tend to rise, not fall.

A behavioral explanation for this finding is as follows. Suppose that the representative investor's forecast of future short rates is biased upward. In this case, the market will excessively discount long bonds, thereby unduly driving down their prices. Therefore, yields on current long-term bonds rise. Because the instantaneous short-term interest rate is determined by the production sector in Xiong and Yan (2009), the spread will also widen. However, the long-term bond is underpriced relative to fundamentals. Therefore over time, the price can be expected to rise, thereby driving down future yields, in contradiction of the expectations hypothesis. The asset pricing literature also attributes the failure of the expectations hypothesis to time varying risk aversion. As discussed above, market aggregation implies that wealth shifts can lead to time varying risk aversion. It may well be that the failure of the expectations hypothesis is driven by both features.

Cochrane and Piazzesi (2005) indicate that a tent-shaped function of three forward rates corresponding to maturities of one, three and five years appears to forecast holding period bond returns of all maturities better than the maturity specific forward spreads. Using simulation analysis, Xiong and Yan (2009) use their model to advance an interesting explanation for the tent-shaped factor. They note that yields to intermediate maturities display the greatest sensitivity to beliefs about l_t. In their parametric specification, the greatest sensitivity occurs at a maturity length of three years, making the three-year forward rate more sensitive than the one year or five year. When wealth shifts to the bullish investor, the representative investor's estimate $\hat{l}_t$ increases, thereby increasing the impact of the three-year forward rate relative to the other two. As a result, the value of the tent-factor increases, because of the disproportionate weight on the three-year forward rate. A higher value for the tent-shaped factor predicts a higher bond return. The higher bond return occurs because, as described above, the bullish investor's beliefs unduly drives down the current price, which mean reverts in the future.

5.6.2 Behavioral Option Pricing

Shefrin (2008a) shows that the linear properties discussed in connection with bond prices also apply to option prices. In particular, Shefrin (2008a) presents a specific example involving heterogenous beliefs in which equilibrium option prices can be represented as wealth-weighted convex combinations of Black–Scholes prices that would apply in homogeneous belief economies.

One of the major empirical features associated with option pricing is the option "smirk" or "smile," which refers to the shape of the implied volatility function (IVF). Given a set of options which vary only by exercise price, the IVF maps the exercise price to the implied volatility derived from applying the Black–Scholes option formula to the market price. If the market treated the return of the underlying security as following a Brownian motion, then the IVF would be flat instead of decreasing (the smirk) or U-shaped (the smile). Notably, the option smirk in the IVF occurs in conjunction with an oscillating SDF, where there is disagreement about investors about the volatility of the asset underlying the options.

Heterogeneity typically prevents equilibrium option prices from satisfying Black–Scholes because heterogeneity leads the risk neutral density to be non-normal. In the continuous time example presented in Shefrin (2008a), the interest rate and volatility that serve as inputs into the Black–Scholes formula are correct. When equilibrium option prices do not satisfy Black–Scholes, it is not because the input values are necessarily incorrect. Black–Scholes fails because the risk-neutral density is non-normal, even though the objective return distribution for the asset underlying the option is normal.

Black–Scholes intuition has developed around partial equilibrium models. In these models, the risk-neutral pdf is derived from an objective normal pdf as a change of measure. In this case, the risk-neutral pdf is itself normal with the same volatility as the objective pdf. In the behavioral framework, the risk-neutral pdf is obtained, not from the objective pdf, but from the representative investor's pdf. In this regard, heterogeneity typically leads the representative investor's pdf to be non normal, even when the objective density is normal.

Smile effects occur in the implied volatility function (IVF) because equilibrium option prices do not obey Black–Scholes. In the continuous time example described in Shefrin (2008a), all investors have common knowledge of the objective volatility, which makes it possible to use that volatility to compute the Black–Scholes value associated with any option. By way of contrast, the IVF backs out volatilities implied by the risk-neutral pdf based on the representative investor's pdf. In the example portrayed in Shefrin (2008a), the representative investor's pdf features greater volatility than the common knowledge volatility, leading the IVF function to lie above its common knowledge counterpart.

The analysis easily extends to the case when investors differ in their views about volatility, although in this case there is a question as to which volatility to use in the Black–Scholes formula. One possibility is to use the volatility associated with the representative investor's pdf. However, the analysis is little changed if the objective volatility were used, or a convex combination of the investors' subjective volatilities.

As I mentioned above, the change of measure used to derive risk-neutral densities from objective densities is based on a behavioral SDF rather than a neoclassical SDF. Therefore, the behavioral risk-neutral density need not feature the same volatility as the objective density, as is the case in neoclassical models.

Much of the empirical work estimating the SDF and market risk aversion is based on index option prices. In this respect, option smiles and smirks and the oscillating shape of the empirical SDF represent different sides of the same coin. To the extent that the sentiment component of the SDF is germane, the same will be true of index option prices. In this regard, Han (2008) finds that changes in sentiment explain time variation in the slope of index option smile which traditional factors cannot. He reports that when market sentiment becomes more bearish, the index IVF smile is steeper and the risk-neutral skewness of monthly index returns is more negative .

Constantinides et al. (2009) examine possible mispricing of SPX options for the periods 1988–1995 and 1997–2002. Their analysis contains some novel elements, specifically the inclusion of transaction costs. Notably, they ask whether market prices were such that in any month of their study, an investor with objectively correct beliefs could have increased his expected utility by engaging in a zero-net-cost trade. They find that there were many months when this would have been possible, thereby leading them to conclude that SPX options were mispriced over time. In particular, they note that mispricing was pronounced for out-of-the-money call options. Interestingly, they suggest that before the crash of 1987, option traders might have navely used the Black–Scholes formula when it did not apply. Doing so corresponds to the use of the formula as a heuristic.

The analysis in Constantinides et al. (2009) implies that the pricing of SPX options cannot be explained in terms of a neoclassical representative investor holding correct beliefs. This analysis neither makes explicit use of sentiment, nor takes into account how sentiment injects oscillation into the shape of the SDF. Nevertheless, the authors implicitly acknowledge sentiment-based explanations for their results.

6

Behavioralizing Corporate Finance

Behavioral corporate finance can be thought of as the intersection of finance and management Gaston-Breton and Lejarraga (2009). The groundwork for behavioral corporate finance was laid out in a series of papers Meir Statman and a series of coauthors wrote about project decisions. See Statman and Tyebjee (1985), Statman and Caldwell (1987), and Statman and Sepe (1989). In Shefrin (2001), I suggested that enough was known about the behavioral aspects of corporate finance to identify a subfield one could label "behavioral corporate finance." Other early contributions included Heaton (2002) and Gervais et al. (2003). Heaton (2002) explored the impact of managerial overconfidence on spending and finance decisions. Gervais et al. (2003) pointed out that overconfidence can exert a positive impact on the value of the firm by mitigating agency conflicts, a point also developed in Goel and Thakor (2008) and Hackbarth (2009).[1]

[1] The framework developed in Hackbarth (2009) is contingent claims based, and should prove especially useful for integrating behavioral corporate issues into a general asset pricing model.

6.1 Open Questions Raised by Baker et al.

In this section, I take as my starting point the behavioral corporate framework developed in Baker et al. (2007b) discussed in Section 2 above. That framework goes a long way toward behavioralizing corporate finance. Baker et al. (2007b) conclude with a series of open questions about the future direction of behavioral corporate finance.

I wrote my behavioral corporate textbook (Shefrin, 2005) at the same time that Baker et al. were writing their survey. I intended my text for classroom instruction, in order to provide a behavioral supplement to the traditional material taught in corporate finance courses. In many ways, the textbook approach parallels the approach in Baker et al. (2007b). In this regard, I call criterion functions such as Equations (2.1) and (2.4) "behavioral adjusted present value." The text offers a series of cases to make the material concrete for students. I suggest that some of the case discussions provide insight into a list of open questions that conclude Baker et al. (2007b).

Debt Puzzle

The first open question in Baker et al. (2007b) asks why managers do not pursue the tax benefits of debt more aggressively, an issue raised by Graham (2000). In Shefrin (2005) I present a case about the pharmaceutical firm Merck, suggesting that the loss aversion property in prospect theory offers a potential explanation, as bankruptcy losses loom much larger than the gains associated with tax shield benefits. In private correspondence, Graham has indicated that he concurs, suggesting that managers do not want to get too close to the edge of the cliff.

Irrational Managers and Inefficient Prices

The second open question asks whether a model that incorporates both irrational managers and inefficient prices would lead to new insights. There is no reason why irrational managers should not balance perceived short-term gains against perceived long-term value. Theoretically, it is straightforward to combine Equations (2.1) and (2.4) in order to capture both phenomena. One way to do this is to modify Equation (2.1), replacing output $f(K;)$ with $(1+\gamma)f(K;)$ from Equation (2.4), and changing the base from which the mispricing term $\delta(\cdot)$ is measured from 0 to $-\gamma f(K;)$. Notably, mispricing is now understood in the sense of "perceived" mispricing. These substitutions lead to the criterion function:

$$\lambda[(1+\gamma)f(K;) - K + (e(\delta(\cdot) - \gamma f(K;)))] + (1-\lambda)[\delta(\cdot) - \gamma f(K;)]. \tag{6.1}$$

As to how the combination of irrational managers and inefficient prices might be germane, in Shefrin (2005) I present a case about the acquisition of Time-Warner by AOL, one of the largest in history. I suggest that the financial features of this case reflect both irrational managers and inefficient prices. In line with the Shleifer–Vishny framework, the executives at AOL did use overvalued equity to purchase Time-Warner. However, Time-Warner's CEO Gerald Levin was not skeptical about mispricing, in contrast to the general evidence presented by Malmendier and Tate (2008).

Debiasing

One of the most important open questions involves debiasing, how corporations can learn to reduce susceptibility to managerial pitfalls? In Shefrin (2005), I devote considerable space to this issue, including a section focusing on the role psychological phenomena play in business process. To be sure, psychological pitfalls might well lead managers to make decisions that are not in the best interests of shareholders. From a neoclassical perspective, this represents an agency conflict, a concept that is already central to corporate finance. However, because the conflict is not between rational principals and rational agents, the usual incentive remedies for traditional agency conflicts may not apply. Indeed there is already a literature in addressing behavioral bias within organizations (Heath et al., 1998).

Shefrin (2005) emphasizes that behavioral phenomena and agency phenomena are both central to corporate finance. There are two main issues involving the relationship between agency phenomena and behavioral phenomena. First, a key challenge is to differentiate them clearly, so behavioral issues do not come to be regarded as rational agency issues. Second, there is a whole behavioral dimension to the treatment of agency phenomena. In Shefrin (2005) I devote a section to discussing interactions between nonrational principals and nonrational agents.

Shefrin (2005) is organized to identify how psychological pitfalls create gaps between recommended courses of action in corporate finance textbooks and what corporate managers actually do. Topics include the spectrum from valuation analysis to real options. The literature on these gaps continues to grow. For example, Tiwana et al. (2007) document a series of cases in which managers make imperfect use of real option analysis. In particular, managers are apt to downplay real option analysis for high NPV projects relative to low NPV projects, thereby underestimating the value of the latter.

Themes in the Remainder of the Section

In the body of this section, I focus on three main issues pertaining to the behavioralization of corporate finance. All relate to delving more deeply into understanding the impact of managers' personality characteristics on their decisions. The first is based on the analysis of surveys to identify the impact of managerial optimism decisions about debt ratios, debt maturity, dividend policy, and acquisition frequency. The second is a study about the impact of social networks to which CEOs belong, especially when it comes to vulnerability to groupthink. The third is evidence about the psychological traits of entrepreneurs, which builds on the discussion in Baker et al. (2007b).

The three themes upon which I focus are not exhaustive. There have been numerous new papers in behavioral corporate finance that build on earlier ideas. Some examples are as follows: Degeorge et al. (2007) document that managers tend to rely on bookbuilding to go public, which is less cost effective than auction techniques. Huang and Ritter (2009) analyze the empirical issues associated with achieving target capital structures. Spalt (2008) studies the degree to which firms use option-based compensation to exploit managerial optimism. Peyer and Vermaelen (2009) establish that the buyback puzzle has not disappeared. Campbell et al. (2009) use turnover rates to test and confirm the predictions in Goel and Thakor (2008) that there is an optimal degree of overconfidence to balance agency conflicts.

6.2 Managerial Psychology and Decisions

6.2.1 Results Based on FEI Survey

Ben-David et al. (2007) provide interesting insights into the connection between overconfidence and managerial decisions. Their study makes use of a survey Duke University and *CFO* magazine jointly run of the members of Financial Executives International (FEI), an association of top financial executives. The survey features a unique panel of nearly 7,000 observations of managers' probability distributions regarding the stock market. Survey results show the financial executives to be miscalibrated: Over a six-year period, realized market returns are within the executives' 80 percent confidence intervals only 38 percent of the time.

Given that raising external capital is costly, firms whose projects have high NPV can do their shareholders a favor by keeping their dividend payouts low, and using the cash to fund projects instead. After all, high NPV means that the company is able to generate higher expected returns through its projects than investors can earn if instead paid the cash. Overconfidence leads executives to underestimate the risk attached to project cash flows, resulting in overestimates of projects' NPV. As a result, the greater the degree of overconfidence, the more inclined are executives to adopt projects, and undertake acquisitions.

Overconfidence can also impact capital structure. Think about unrealistically optimistic, overconfident managers seeking to balance the tax shield benefits of debt against the expected costs of financial distress, especially bankruptcy. They will be inclined to underestimate the likelihood of going into bankruptcy, and therefore to underestimate the expected cost bankruptcy. Therefore, overconfident managers will be prone to take on more debt than is appropriate.

The general evidence from the Ben-David et al. (2007) is that the greater the degree of unrealistic optimism and overconfidence on the part of executives, the more prone they are to take on excessive debt. In the Duke/FEI survey, the average debt ratio was 23 percent. Imagine dividing executives into ten groups according to their overconfidence. Suppose that for each group, we compute the average debt ratio of the company that the executive works for. Ben-David et al. (2007) report that as we migrate from the group having the lowest overconfidence to the group having the highest overconfidence, the debt ratio increases by 0.5 percent every time we move up to a new group.

In addition, overconfident executives tend to take out debt with longer maturities. The average maturity for the survey firms was 3.7 years. However, the group with the highest overconfidence rating took out longer loans than the group with the lowest overconfidence rating, by about one year. The longer maturity leaves a company with less financial flexibility, and more interest rate risk.

6.2.2 Results Based on Personality Tests

Graham et al. (2009) may well be the first study which measures attitudes of senior management directly through personality tests and then relates the results to firm level policies such as the usage of debt and mergers and acquisitions. In 2006, the authors surveyed both CEOs and CFOs. Most of the executives surveyed were identified as readers of *Chief Executive*, *CFO magazine*, and for CFOs the publications *CFO Europe* and *CFO Asia* magazines. The responses generated a database with 1,180 CEOs with 1,017 CEOs who work for firms headquartered in the United States. For CFOs, there were correspondingly 549 responses.

In their survey, Graham et al. (2009) elicit responses to indicate degree of risk aversion, dispositional optimism, time preference, and aversion to a sure loss. To assess risk aversion, the authors use a procedure developed by Barsky et al. (1997). To assess optimism, they administer a standard psychometric test known as Scheier and Carvers Life Orientation Test Revised or LOT-R test. To measure time preferences, they assess time predilection for gains and losses. To gauge aversion to a sure loss, they present managers with a gamble that, if taken, indicates that the survey respondent is averse to a sure loss. In addition, Graham et al. (2009) elicit other measures that be related, such as height as a measure of confidence, age, tenure, career track, education, and prestige of the executives undergraduate college.

In respect to debt, Graham et al. (2009) report that CEOs with a background in finance and accounting tend to take on more debt than CEO with other backgrounds. This might be a reflection of the availability heuristic, as managers with formal backgrounds in finance and accounting will be more familiar with the advantages of debt. Interestingly, males, optimists, and executives from private companies are more likely to use a higher proportion of short term debt than others. See Landier and Thesmar (2009) whose theory suggests that optimists are more likely to take on short-term debt. If male gender is positively correlated with overconfidence, as suggested by Barber and Odean (2000), then overconfidence appears to lead to more usage of short-term debt.

Graham et al. (2009) find that CEOs who are more risk tolerant are also more likely to make acquisitions, as are CEOs who are averse to a sure loss. There may be several explanations for the second finding. In Shefrin (2005) I suggest that the managers of poorly performing firms, who register subpar performance as a psychological loss, are prone to engage in risky acquisition activity. Graham et al. (2009) point out that managers who are averse to a sure loss are more prone to engage in multiple acquisitions, perhaps because they keep bidding until they win.

Interpreting height as a measure of confidence, the results in Graham et al. (2009) suggest a matching story whereby young, confident, risk-tolerant CEOs are more likely to work for high growth companies and companies with high anticipated growth rates. In terms of relying on incentive-based compensation, three personal characteristics appear to be significant: risk-taking, gender, and rate of time preference. Graham et al. (2009) find that risk-tolerant CEOs are more likely to obtain proportionately larger remuneration through incentives such as stock, bonus payments, and option grants relative to a large salary. In this regard, Spalt (2008) reports a complementary finding, that some firms use stock option pay for lower-level employees to take advantage of biased probability judgments or weightings. Not surprisingly, males are more likely to be compensated through incentives, as are executives who are more patient. Moreover, Graham et al. (2009) hypothesize that firms set compensation policies to hire managers who, over time, will perpetuate corporate policies, such as capital structure.

An intriguing finding of Graham et al. (2009) involves the benchmarking of the dispositional optimism of U.S. CEOs against others. On a 0–4 range, the average response for the general population is about 2.5. However, more than 80 percent of CEOs' responses to the optimism questions average about 3, so that CEOs are significantly more optimistic than the lay population.

CEOs are also more optimistic than CFOs, with only 66 percent of CFOs being classified as very optimistic. Interestingly, when asked to rate CEO optimism relative to their own, CFOs confirm this finding. CFO suggests that CEOs are more optimistic about all aspects of life, not just business prospects. There are other ways CEOs differ from CFOs. CEOs are less likely to have MBA degrees than CFOs. CEOs are likely to be older, have longer tenure, and to have attended more prestigious universities. Strikingly, CFOs are more averse to sure losses and more patient than CEOs.

Finally, Graham et al. (2009) report that both CEOs and CFOs from the United States are more risk tolerant than the CEOs and CFOs of 25 companies which are not located in the United States. In addition, non-U.S. CEOs and CFOs are less patient than their U.S. counterparts. Foreign CEOs also have a higher aversion to sure losses than do U.S. CEOs.

6.3 Social Networks

Fracassi and Tate (2009) test whether connections, in the sense of social networks, between management and potential directors influence director selection and subsequent firm performance.[2] Their study uses panel data for firms in the S&P 1500, thereby focusing on social ties in large U.S. corporations. In this respect, Fracassi and Tate (2009) identify directors who belong (or belonged) to the same golf clubs, charities, and other non-professional organizations as the CEO. They consider employees' histories, identifying directors who, with the exception of the current firm, were employed by the same firm as the CEO in the

[2] Studies focusing on social networking are gaining interest. See Cai and Sevilir (2009) and Ishii and Xuan (2009) who study the role of social networks involving directors and/or managers in M&A.

past. Finally, they identify directors who attended the same educational institutions as the CEO.

In Shefrin (2005), I discuss a series of psychological impediments to effective governance processes. A key impediment is "groupthink" (Janis, 1972; Bénabou, 2008). Groupthink is a form of collective confirmation bias for groups, whereby there is insufficient dissent within the group, resulting in the amplification of individual biases. Groupthink can result when group members are too similar to one another, all sharing similar perspectives. Therefore, close ties between the CEO and the board, based on similarities in backgrounds and experiences, increase the potential for groupthink. In this regard, Fracassi and Tate (2009) point out that directors might be more willing to give the benefit of the doubt to management when they have a closer relationship with, and trust in, the CEO.

In Shefrin (2005), I point out that when it comes to heterogeneous board composition, some boards might look good on paper, yet be very vulnerable to groupthink. Indeed U.S. exchanges require the majority of directors in listed firms to be independent, and in recent years have strengthened independence requirements for key board committees. Alas, this is no guarantee that directors with network connections to the CEO qualify as independent directors, but are not unbiased monitors.

Social Connectivity and Firm Value

Fracassi and Tate (2009) find that the relationship between social connectivity and firm value, measured using Tobin's Q, is negative. Moreover, the effect is strongest when shareholder rights are weak. In the remainder of this section, I discuss some of the specific issues associated with the negative relationship.

Consider alternative measures of CEO power such as being both board chair and president, long tenure, a high entrenchment index, and being much more highly paid than the next best paid executive. Fracassi and Tate (2009) report that CEOs who are powerful are prone to add new directors having existing network ties to the CEO. Such directors are more likely to buy company stock at the same time as the

CEO. Specifically, relative to other outside directors, directors closely connected to the CEO through social networks are more likely to purchase stock within five days of a CEO stock purchase. In addition, if the CEO is a net buyer, then over the fiscal year these directors are more likely to be net buyers.

More importantly, there is some evidence that the presence of directors closely connected to the CEO is correlated with weaker monitoring. For example, firms with closely connected directors are less likely to initiate earnings restatements which are internally prompted. Especially, interesting is the fact that firms with boards closely connected to the CEO make more frequent acquisitions. Fracassi and Tate (2009) state that the merger bids of these firms destroy \$407 million of shareholder value on average, \$293 million more than the bids of other firms. This feature complements the discussion in the prior section about the characteristics of CEOs of firms who are frequent acquirers.

Not surprisingly, such poor decisions lead to lower overall market valuations, especially when shareholder rights are weak when it comes to substituting for board monitoring. Specifically, Fracassi and Tate (2009) find that the average cumulative abnormal return for the three-day window surrounding merger announcements is lower for firms with a higher percentage of connected directors. They also find that the average value created by the deals (for acquiring shareholders) is negative, and that the value destruction is concentrated in firms with weak shareholder rights as measured by Gompers et al. (2003).

Plausibly, acquisition-based value destruction might well reflect a monitoring failure or an advisory failure on the part of the board. Major acquisitions might be initiated by the CEO; however, they require board approval. Directors connected to the CEO might be unwilling to oppose value-destroying policies that provide private benefits to the CEO. Alternatively, such directors might withhold information in their possession that does not support the CEO's proposal.

Fracassi and Tate (2009) indicate that their analysis does not provide much insight into the motivation of connected independent directors. They identify several possibilities. For example, connected directors might be seeking to expedite the CEO's agenda, in which case they are complicit in the associated value destruction. Alternatively, connected directors might be motivated by an interest in preserving social ties with the CEO. Finally, connected directors might simply share the CEO's perspective, or cognitive biases, by dint of having the same background and moving in the same social circles.

6.4 Entrepreneurs

This section has two goals.[3] The first goal is to broaden the psychological framework used to characterize managers. The second goal is to identify the psychological profile of entrepreneurs with the goal of understanding why they tolerate inferior returns. In this respect, the discussion about the psychological profile of entrepreneurs will serve as a vehicle for both goals.

Shefrin (2005) and Baker et al. (2007b) both indicate that among the many psychological phenomena, behavioral corporate finance mainly focuses on excessive optimism and overconfidence. In this respect, I note that the behavioral decision literature does not treat these concepts as primitives, but identifies factors that explain what makes people excessively optimistic and overconfident. A key factor is control. Weinstein (1980) and Flynn et al. (1994) indicate that control is a determinant of both excessive optimism and overconfidence. Below I discuss how psychologists measure control, and relate the discussion to entrepreneurs.

Baker et al. (2007b) devote several paragraphs to entrepreneurs. This is because entrepreneurs appear to accept inferior returns. Hamilton (2000) establishes that entrepreneurs accept lower median lifetime earnings than similarly skilled wage-earners. Moskowitz and Vissing-Jorgensen (2002) establish that entrepreneurs earn low risk-adjusted returns.[4] Moreover, entrepreneurs appear to hold poorly diversified portfolios. Instead they concentrate their wealth in their own private business (Gentry and Hubbard, 2001; Moskowitz and Vissing-Jorgensen, 2002; Heaton and Lucas, 2000). In light of the

[3] I draw the material for this section from Shefrin (2010).

[4] The average return to all private equity is actually similar to that of the public market equity index. However, the risk is higher. Survival rates of private firms are only around 34 percent over the first 10 years of the firms life.

evidence, Bitler et al. (2004) investigate the structuring of incentives for entrepreneurs and ask why people would choose to become entrepreneurs.

Puri and Robinson (2008) provide some insight into why people would choose to become entrepreneurs. They ask whether entrepreneurs are risk-takers. They suggest that entrepreneurs might derive substantial non-pecuniary benefits from self-employment. Based on their prior work (Puri and Robinson, 2007), they hypothesize that entrepreneurs might be optimistic about their entrepreneurial prospects. Puri and Robinson's analysis of the data in the Survey of Consumer Finances (SCF) leads them to a series of conclusions. First, they find that entrepreneurs are more risk-loving and optimistic than the rest of the population. Second, these traits are separable in that the correlation between risk tolerance and optimism is low. Third, entrepreneurs tend to have long planning horizons, good health practices, and strong family ties. In respect to planning, entrepreneurs are almost three times more likely to indicate that they never intend to retire. Moreover, people who do not plan to retire work about 3 percent longer per week. In the main, these findings are supported by Wadhwa et al. (2009).

Consider how the configuration of entrepreneurs' characteristics relates to the suboptimality of the returns which they earn. Unless entrepreneurs are actually risk seeking, being more risk-loving than the general population does not explain why entrepreneurs earn suboptimal risk-adjusted returns. Notably, optimism might provide part of the explanation. Puri and Robinson focus on dispositional optimism as opposed to unrealistic optimism. They point out that the psychology literature distinguishes between dispositional optimism and optimistic bias. The former views optimism as a positive personality trait associated with positive generalized expectations of the future (Scheier and Carver, 1985). The latter views optimism as a negative, domain-specific bias in expectations (Weinstein, 1980).

It is straightforward to see how optimistic bias can lead to inferior returns. Of course, dispositional optimism can also involve optimistic bias, and therefore produce inferior returns as well. This is not to say that the net impact of dispositional optimism is negative. In this regard, Bitler et al. (2004) find that effort increases firm performance. In their analysis, Puri and Robinson focus on dispositional optimism. They do not measure optimism bias directly, but infer it from self-reported estimates of own life expectancy. Shefrin (2010) extends their analysis by surveying entrepreneurs for dispositional optimism and comparing their responses with the responses of non-entrepreneurs.

While the combination of risk-seeking choices and optimism possibly explains why entrepreneurs earn low risk-adjusted returns, it seems far more plausible that non-pecuniary benefits lie at the heart of the issue. After all, entrepreneurs work longer hours and plan to retire later than their non-entrepreneur counterparts. What might those non-pecuniary benefits be? I suggest that a major non-pecuniary benefit for entrepreneurs is the exercise of control over their working environment, the control that derives from starting a new business and managing that business. In this regard, I hypothesize that the desire for control is a psychological need which might be higher for entrepreneurs than non-entrepreneurs.

Puri and Robinson document that relative to non-entrepreneurs, entrepreneurs are more likely to be married and have larger families (see also Wadhwa et al., 2009). This suggests that entrepreneurs might be more socially focused than others. I hypothesize that this is the case. In particular, I test whether entrepreneurs are less anxious in social settings than non-entrepreneurs, and more aware of social cues and their own behavior.

If entrepreneurs derive significant non-pecuniary benefits from entrepreneurial activity, then it seems plausible that entrepreneurs would report being happier than their non-entrepreneurial counterparts. I test whether this is the case using two instruments, one pertaining to well-being (life satisfaction) and the other pertaining to degree of affect (positive, neutral, or negative). The major findings are as follows: entrepreneurs exhibit more dispositional optimism than their non-entrepreneurial counterparts. Notably, the most significant difference between entrepreneurs and non-entrepreneurs is the desire for control: entrepreneurs place much more emphasis on control. Entrepreneurs appear to be more comfortable in social situations, and feel that they are more sensitive to social cues. They also report being more positive and more satisfied with their lives. Taken together, these findings suggest that the non-pecuniary benefits that entrepreneurs experience are substantial.

6.4.1 Data

The data for this study involve responses to a series of psychological surveys. The surveys relate to instruments for measuring dispositional optimism (Scheier and Carver, 1985), desirability of control (Burger and Cooper, 1979), social anxiousness (Leary, 1983), self-monitoring behavior (Snyder, 1974; Lennox and Wolfe, 1984), life satisfaction (Diener et al., 1985), and affect (Watson and Clark, 1988). The surveys were administered to two different groups: (1) a group of entrepreneurs and (2) a group of MBA and undergraduate business students (non-entrepreneurs).

6.4.2 Desire for Control

Puri and Robinson classify respondents to the SCF as entrepreneurs if they own some or all of at least one privately owned business, and are full-time self-employed. It seems plausible to suggest that people who fit this description exert more control over their working environment than others, and that part of the appeal of being an entrepreneur is achieving this degree of control. Put somewhat differently, entrepreneurs possess a strong need for control which leads them to choose a career in which they seek to meet that need. This statement reflects a view in the literature on motivation about the importance of nonmonetary rewards relative to monetary rewards.

Burger and Cooper (1979) introduce a survey instrument (DC) which is designed to measure the desirability of control. The survey instrument consists of twenty questions. Two representative questions are: "I prefer a job where I have a lot of control over what I do and when I do it," and "I would prefer to be a leader than a follower." The range of possible responses varies from 1 to 7 where 1 means "The statement does not apply to me at all," and 7 means "The statement always applies to me." For 15 of the questions, 7 is associated with the strongest desire for control, while for 5 of the questions, 1 is associated with the strongest desire for control. For sake of consistency, the score for each of the 5 questions is replaced by 7-score.

The results suggest that desire for control is a major non-pecuniary benefit associated with being an entrepreneur. The average DC score per question is 5.4 for entrepreneurs and 4.6 for non-entrepreneurs. To interpret these results, note that 4 means "I am unsure about whether or not the statement applies to me or it applies to me about half the time," 5 means "The statement applies more often than not," and 6 means "The statement usually applies to me."

6.4.3 Optimism

Using their life expectancy proxy for optimism, Puri and Robinson find that entrepreneurs exhibit more dispositional optimism than non-entrepreneurs. I augment their analysis by using an instrument to measure dispositional optimism (Scheier and Carver, 1985).

The optimism instrument (OP) consists of eight questions whose responses fall on a five-point scale where 1 means "strongly disagree" and 5 means "strongly agree." Two of the questions are: "I'm always optimistic about my future," and "I hardly ever expect things to go my way."

Adjusting for signs, the mean OP-score for entrepreneurs was 3.5 and for non-entrepreneurs it was 3.2. Notably, both groups feature OP-scores between Neutral and Agree, and are therefore optimistic. Although entrepreneurs appear to be more optimistic than non-entrepreneurs, the difference in scores is not statistically significant for the particular sample in my study. However, the results are quite similar to the larger sample described in Puri and Robinson (2008), where the differences are statistically significant.

6.4.4 Social Anxiousness and Self-monitoring

Consider psychological attributes which relate to the finding that entrepreneurs marry at a higher rate than non-entrepreneurs and have more children. This finding suggests that entrepreneurs like people. This subsection considers two psychological instruments that relate to interpersonal relationships. The first stems from the work of Leary (1983), who studied social anxiousness, the degree to which people are uncomfortable in social situations. The second relates to self-monitoring, a concept studied by Snyder (1974) and Lennox and Wolfe (1984).

The survey instrument used to study social anxiousness (SA) features fifteen questions. Two of the questions are: "I often feel nervous even in casual get-togethers," and "I get nervous when I speak to someone in a position of authority." Responses are on a 5-point scale where 1 means "Not at all characteristic," and 5 means "Extremely characteristic."

A lower SA score signals less social anxiety. Entrepreneurs have a mean SA score of 2.0, whereas non-entrepreneurs' mean SA score is 2.9. A score of 2 means "Slightly characteristic" and a score of 3 means "Moderately characteristic."

Self-monitoring involves being sensitive to social cues, and being able to adapt to those cues. The self-monitoring survey instrument is SM. It features questions such as the following: "I am often able to read people's true emotions correctly through their eyes." "In social situations, I have the ability to alter my behavior if I feel something else is called for." The range of possible responses comprises a 6-point scale from "Always false" to "Always true."

The mean score for entrepreneurs is 4.4 and for non-entrepreneurs is 3.9. Here 3 means "Somewhat false, but with exception," 4 means "Somewhat true, but with exception," and 5 means "Generally true."

6.4.5 Affect and Well-Being

Are entrepreneurs happier than non-entrepreneurs? What makes this question especially interesting is that entrepreneurs work more than non-entrepreneurs and earn lower risk-adjusted returns on their investments. To investigate the question, I use survey instruments based on the work of Watson and Clark (1988), who study affect, and Diener et al. (1985), who study life satisfaction or well-being. I refer to the associated instruments as AF and WB, respectively.

The affect survey asks respondents to indicate how frequently they experience a variety of emotional states such as "interested," "distressed," and "excited." Responses are on a 5-point scale, in which 1 means "very slightly or not at all," and 5 means "extremely." Some states connote negative affect and some connote positive affect. An AF score of zero connotes neutral overall affect. The mean AF-score for entrepreneurs was 1.2 and the mean AF-score for non-entrepreneurs was 0.8.

The life satisfaction survey asks respondents twenty-five true/false questions such as "I always seem to have something pleasant to look forward to," and "Often I get irritated at little annoyances." Of the 25 questions, 11 relate to feelings of positive life satisfaction and 14 to negative feelings. Relative to an adjusted neutral score of 0, the mean WB-score for entrepreneurs was −1.0 and for non-entrepreneurs was −1.2. Entrepreneurs score higher on the WB-survey. However, both groups' mean scores are negative responses. Overall, the evidence indicates that entrepreneurs are happier than non entrepreneurs.

6.4.6 Risk Preferences

Puri and Robinson (2008) find that entrepreneurs are more risk-loving and optimistic than the rest of the population, although the correlation between risk tolerance and optimism is low. The analysis suggests that desire for control is a major motivator for why people choose to be entrepreneurs, stronger than optimism, and perhaps risk attitude as well. In terms of risk, it is possible that people choose to be entrepreneurs because they have a preference for lottery-type returns. To test for this possibility, I ran a supplementary survey, based on the concepts in SP/A theory (see Section 3) which posed the following two questions to entrepreneurs:

1. On a scale of 1 to 7 where 1 is unimportant and 7 is extremely important, how important to you is upside potential as a reason being an entrepreneur?
2. On a scale of 1 to 7 where 1 is unimportant and 7 is extremely important, how important to you is being in control of your work world as a reason being an entrepreneur?

The mean response to the first question was 5.8 and to the second was 6.3. Clearly, both factors are important. However, between the two, control is more important.

The supplementary survey also posed qualitative questions designed to elicit features emphasized by SP/A theory, such as the strength of emotions such as fear and hope, and whether entrepreneurs establish specific aspirational goals. These respectively correspond to the three main variables in the theory, S, P, and A. The responses indicate that entrepreneurs feel that fear is a weak emotion for them, hope is a moderately strong emotion, and aspirational goals are strong. Many indicate that they would accept lottery-type returns if the downside is small, but are more reluctant if the downside is not small, if doing so significantly diminishes the probability of achieving their specific aspirations.

7

Behavioralizing the Approach to Financial Market Regulation

The behavioral aspect of financial market regulation is a particularly rich area of study. A major reason why is its complexity, in that it combines behavioral aspects of portfolio selection, derivatives, asset pricing, corporate finance, and political economy. Yet, until the global financial crisis erupted in 2008, financial economists paid little attention to financial market regulation in general and its behavioral aspects in particular.

To the best of my knowledge, the first behavioral treatment of financial market regulation is found in Shefrin and Statman (1992, 1993b). The literature then lay dormant until Hirshleifer (2008b), who was unaware of our earlier work, and addressed some of the same issues. Statman (2009) and Shefrin and Statman (2009) describe how their framework applies to a series of issues preceding and including the financial crisis. The series includes credit card and bank regulations, the evolution of insider trading regulations, Regulation FD, trading halts, the Global Settlement, and the Sarbanes–Oxley Act.

In this section, I review the basic behavioral approach to financial market regulation, with reference to both historical and recent financial crises.

7.1 Dynamic Tug-of-War

7.1.1 Fairness and Efficiency

The regulation of financial markets in the United States can only be understood in reference to the continuous debate that has shaped it. In this respect, financial market regulation reflects concerns for both efficiency and fairness, a point emphasized by Shefrin and Statman (1992).[1] Regulations are the outcome of a dynamic tug-of-war between parties with differing views about efficiency and fairness, in which relative strength continually shifts from side to side.

There are two notions of efficiency in financial economics. The first is Pareto efficiency and the second is informational efficiency. An allocation is said to be Pareto efficient when no other feasible allocation of resources and technology can improve one person's situation without harming another's. By its nature, Pareto efficiency precludes the wasting of resources. It also ensures that the riskiness of investment projects are in line with the attitudes of investors toward risk. Notably, Pareto efficiency is consistent with errors and biases. In a Pareto-efficient allocation, investors might well take on more risk than is objectively appropriate or overreact to information and cause security prices to be excessively volatile.

Informational efficiency is achieved when all investors share objective beliefs and information so that competitive prices accurately reflect that information. Efficient prices provide proper guidance to entrepreneurs, managers, and investors. By observing prices, managers can avoid projects with negative net present value, and investors can select efficient portfolios. However, some managers and investors might misinterpret the information conveyed within efficient prices and make supoptimal choices. Asymmetric information destroys informational efficiency and moral hazard interferes with it.

Shefrin and Statman (1992) build on Kahneman et al. (1991), who provided the first behavioral characterization of fairness in terms of "reference transactions." Shefrin and Statman (1992) propose that in financial markets fairness is understood as entitlements to particular

[1] This section is drawn from some of the main ideas in Shefrin and Statman (1992, 1993b).

classes of transactions. They identify seven classes of fairness by the following entitlements:

— A transaction is fair when the parties enter into it voluntarily. Freedom from coercion entitles people to avoid being coerced into a transaction against their will, and being permitted to engage in a transaction of their choosing.
— Freedom from misrepresentation entitles people to rely on voluntarily disclosed information being accurate.
— Fairness in equal information entitles people to equal access to a particular set of information.
— Fairness in equal processing power entitles people not only to equal access to information but also to a "competency floor" of information processing skills. This class of fairness recognizes that some people commit cognitive errors. Protecting them may take the form of compulsory disclosure or the outright prohibition of certain types of transactions.
— Fairness as freedom from impulse entitles people to protection from possible imperfect self-control.
— Fairness in efficient prices entitles people to prices they perceive to be efficient. This is the notion of fairness inherent in the term "fair and orderly market."
— Fairness in equal bargaining power entitles people to equal power in negotiations leading to a transaction. Bargaining power inequality can occur, for example, when one party to a transaction is wealthier than the other.

Policymakers operate as if they have preferences which depend on both efficiency and fairness. Some combinations of efficiency and fairness dominate other combinations that are higher in one or the other attribute. A conceptual efficiency/fairness frontier is composed of combinations that are not dominated. Choices along the frontier involve reductions in fairness to increase fairness or reductions in fairness to increase efficiency.

7.1.2 Capture Theory

Shefrin and Statman (2009) augment the framework described above to reflect capture theory. This theory postulates that interest groups regularly enlist politicians and regulators in their battles with one another over regulatory proposals. See Stigler (1971) who noted that each interest group — bankers, lawyers, union members, and employers — wants regulations that maximize its wealth. Politicians have the power to direct regulators to benefit one interest group or another. At the same time, politicians need resources such as campaign contributions to maximize their chances of re-election. Similarly, regulators want to steer the regulatory process in directions that benefit them, in prestige or industry jobs once they leave public service. The political process involves competition among interest groups each attempting to capture politicians and regulators by some combination of votes, contributions, and favors in exchange for enacting and executing regulations which transfer wealth to them.

Stigler emphasized that an interest group is likely to capture its regulators when the per-capita benefits to the members of the interest group are large relative to per-capita benefits to the general public. Peltzman (1976) augmented capture theory, noting that interest groups would not capture their regulators when the total benefits to the general public are sufficiently large, even if the per-capita benefits are relatively small. Politicians and regulators who allow interest groups to capture them under such circumstances might lose more political support than they gain. Politicians and regulators have limited power to tilt regulation toward interest groups and their power varies by the environment in which they operate. Economic booms and rising financial markets placate the general public, reducing its vigilance and making it easier for politicians to tilt regulations toward interest groups. However, recessions and declining financial markets enrage the general public, increasing its vigilance and its clamor for regulatory protection from interest groups. Public outrage is a fire which must be hot enough for a period long enough to shape regulations into a form that benefits the general public. Stoking the fire of public outrage is often difficult because the cost of public mobilization is relatively high. In contrast,

interest groups have ready mechanisms for lobbying which they can mobilize quickly to take advantage of even small changes in the economic, financial, political, legal, and technological environments.

7.1.3 Specific Regulations

Conceptually, each configuration of regulations gives rise to a configuration in efficiency/fairness space. Each regulation is on the frontier unless another regulation improves both fairness and efficiency. Shefrin and Statman (1992) discuss six specific regulations, placing each into the historical context which led the regulations being established. The discussion below emphasizes how the essential issues in the debates can be viewed through the lens of tradeoffs involving differing notions of efficiency and fairness. Shefrin and Statman (1992) emphasize the issues of fairness loom large at the time the regulations were put in place.

1. Merit ("blue-sky") regulations: These diminish Pareto efficiency by restricting choices of those offering and those buying securities. Merit regulations may cause deviations from informationally efficient prices, thus adversely affecting the right to correct (efficient) prices. As to fairness, merit regulation interferes with the right to freedom from coercion, but its paternalistic characteristics enhance rights to equal processing power freedom from impulse. Merit regulations take power from entrepreneurs and give it to investors, a move toward equal power if entrepreneurs have more power than do investors in a mandatory disclosure environment.
2. Disclosure regulations: These improve informational efficiency relative to a buyer beware world. Less clear is whether mandatory disclosure improves Pareto efficiency, on account of its costs, and the potential elimination of some risky ventures. The implications of disclosure regulations for fairness are similar to those for merit regulation.
3. Margin regulations: In the deliberations leading up to the passage of the 1934 Securities Exchange Act, three distinct motivations can be seen underlying the regulation of margin: the need to protect investors from their own

poor judgment, the limitation of price volatility induced by low-margin requirements, and the desire to allocate credit to productive investment instead of financial speculation. The associated issues involve freedom from coercion, efficient prices (fair and orderly markets), equal processing power, and freedom from impulse.

4. Insider trading regulations: The efficiency aspects associated with these regulations pertain to adverse selection. Some argue that the regulations improve informational efficiency, while others argue the opposite, that insiders create new information when they trade. This issue is largely one of timing, however, because most material information is released to the public eventually. The fairness question has played a more prominent part in the debate than the efficiency question, particularly as to a disclosure-or-abstain rule. Two fairness threads can be seen one involving the right to equal information, and the other involving the right to be protected from one's own mistakes. The former issue, which centers on the notion of the "level playing field," has been the more prominent of the two. A fair investment game is perceived to be a similar game of skill, with equal access to public information from which the investor can infer which securities are undervalued and which are overvalued. In a fair game of skill, winners and losers are expected, but trading on inside information is unfair because it conveys a non-skill-based advantage to one party in the trade.
5. Suitability regulations: Suitability rules present a clear case where some fairness rights win over other rights and over efficiency. A move from a no-paternalism to a full-paternalism world enhances the right to freedom from cognitive errors and the right to freedom from impulse. The paternalistic nature of suitability rules is evident in the incentives they provide to brokers to err on the side of low risk rather than on the side of high expected returns.
6. Trading interruption regulations which followed the stock market crash of 1987: trading halts are detrimental to Pareto

efficiency because they prevent parties from entering into agreements viewed as beneficial to themselves. A counter-argument is that trading halts enhance efficiency during a sharp decline by permitting settling up to ensure that all parties are solvent. Any impact on informational efficiency depends on whether such efficiency is achieved in the absence of interruptions. One critic notes that natural trading interruptions, such as the closing bell on the exchange, apparently do not dampen volatility during turbulent periods. As to fairness, the main issues involve coercion, efficient prices (fair and orderly markets), equal information processing, freedom from impulse, and equal bargaining power.

7.1.4 Theoretical Example

7.1.4.1 Absence of Constraints

To fix ideas, consider a numerical binomial example, a special case of the framework described in Section 5, where $T = 2$. Let aggregate consumption be equal to 100 units at $t = 0$. Thereafter the growth rate of aggregate consumption per period is stochastic, and is equal either to $u > 1$ or $d = 1/u < 1$. I take $u = 1.05$, so that the economy grows either at 5 percent per period or shrinks at 4.76 percent. Let there be two types of investors in the model, called type 1 and type 2, with type 1 holding 65 percent of the initial wealth of the economy.

Both types of investors share a common rate of time preference ($\delta = 0.99$). However, the two types of investors differ in their beliefs. Type 1 investors believe that at $t = 1$, the probability that u occurs is 0.8, whereas type 2 investors believe that the probability is 0.67. For $t > 2$, type 1 investors believe that the probability that a u follows a u is 0.95 and that a d follows a d is 0.8. In contrast, type 2 investors believe that aggregate consumption growth evolves according to a process that is independent and identically distributed (i.i.d.), with the probability of u being 0.76 at all dates. For the sake of argument, assume that type 2 investors are information traders, meaning they possess correct beliefs. In this case, type 1 investors will be excessively optimistic after economic growth has been positive and excessively pessimistic after economic growth has been negative, reflecting "hot hand fallacy."

At the beginning of each date, investors decide how to divide their portfolio wealth into current consumption and an end of period portfolio such that the value of consumption together with the end-of-period portfolio is equal to the value of the beginning of period portfolio.

Because the example is binomial, only two securities are needed to complete the market, which I take to be the market portfolio and the one-period risk-free security. In equilibrium, the market portfolio returns 6.1 percent at $t = 1$ if the economy has grown and -3.8 percent if it contracts. At $t = 1$, the interest rate is 3.5 percent. (Returns are calculated using Equation (5.1), as the SDF embodies all price information. Keep in mind that in this model, the market portfolio corresponds to unlevered equity, unlike, say, the S&P 500.)

At $t = 0$, type 1 investors have total wealth equal to \$193, and type 2 investors have total wealth equal to \$104. Both types save 66.3 percent of their wealth and consume the remainder. At the end of $t = 0$, type 1 investors borrow \$314.6 and hold \$442.7 of the market portfolio. Their equity holdings amount to 346 percent of the value of their portfolios. Put another way, type 1 investors purchase 71 percent of their equity holdings on margin. When debt is exclusively used to purchase equity, the degree of margin corresponds to the debt-to-equity ratio. Type 2 investors hold \$314.6 of the risk-free security, and take a short position of $-$\$245.7 in the market portfolio.

At $t = 0$, type 1 investors are more optimistic than type 2 investors, which is why they use leverage to increase their holdings of the market portfolio. Type 1 investors believe that the expected return on the market is 4.1 percent, and therefore the equity premium is 0.6 percent. In contrast, type 2 investors short the market. They believe that the equity premium is -0.7 percent.

The differences in beliefs at $t = 0$ lead to an equilibrium with nonzero sentiment Λ. Notably, equilibrium returns are established as if the market overestimates the probability of an up-move by 12 percent, and underestimates the probability of a down-move by 31 percent. As Equation (5.1) indicates, nonzero sentiment impacts the SDF underlying equilibrium returns.

If growth is positive at $t = 1$, type 1 investors will earn high returns from their levered portfolios. They will increase their consumption by 11.3 percent. In contrast, type 2 investors will decrease their consumption by 6.8 percent.

If growth is negative at $t = 1$, type 1 investors will earn low returns from their levered portfolios. They will decrease their consumption by 22 percent. In contrast, type 2 investors will increase their consumption by 28 percent.

In an example featuring more periods, type 2 investors alternate between acting as if they are excessively optimistic and excessively pessimistic. Volatile beliefs translate into excessive trading. For this reason, some investors might jump from holding portfolios that feature too much leverage to shorting the market portfolio, and back again. For example, if aggregate consumption declines at $t = 1$, type 1 investors will become pessimistic and short \$882 of the market portfolio, while holding \$987 of the risk-free security. In this situation, type 2 investors will end up holding levered positions. These contrasting portfolios reflect contrasting beliefs about the equity premium. After a down move at $t = 1$, type 1 investors believe that the equity premium is -1.9 percent, whereas type 2 investors believe it to be 2.7 percent.

This example illustrates that investors who hold incorrect beliefs choose non-optimal portfolios that feature inappropriate risk exposure and excessive trading. This state of affairs may well occur even when sentiment is zero and prices are efficient. If prices are inefficient, then sentiment typically induces excessive volatility in the market risk premium, thereby exacerbating the degree of non-optimality.

7.1.4.2 Regulatory Constraints, Fairness, and Efficiency

In this framework, financial market regulation operates by imposing constraints on investor's portfolios. For example, regulation can limit leverage and short sales by imposing upper and lower bounds on the portfolio proportion allocated to the market portfolio. The intent of such limits is to force investors to act as if their beliefs were less extreme. From a modeling perspective, the impact of regulations induces investors to act as they hold different beliefs than they actually do, say $\{Q_i\}$ instead of $\{P_i\}$. As in Section 5, a change of measure captures the essential issue. Notably, such constraints typically impact market prices, for example by reducing the degree of volatility in the equity premium.

To see the effect of the change of measure, I modify the example as follows. Consider what happens if economic growth is positive at $t = 1$. In this case, type 1 investors increase their estimate of the equity premium to 1 percent (from 0.6 percent at $t = 0$), and increase the amount of equity purchased on margin to 88 percent (from 71 percent at the end of $t = 0$).

Suppose a regulator, concerned that the market was irrationally exuberant at $t = 0$, were to step in and limit the degree to which investors can purchase equity on margin to 50 percent in all subsequent periods. What difference would this make to investors' positions, imputed beliefs, and market prices? At both $t = 0$ and $t = 1$ after an up-move, type 1 investors would reduce the amount of equity they purchase on margin to 50 percent. At $t = 1$ after a down move, type 2 investors would do likewise. The higher margin requirements would force type 1 investors to trade at $t = 0$ as if they assigned a probability of 72 percent to an up-move at $t = 1$, rather than their true belief of 80 percent. In turn, this would decrease the volatility of the equity premium. At $t = 1$, the ex post premium would be either 1.9 percent or -4.1 percent instead of 2.6 percent or 7.3 percent. The objective expected premium would increase from -0.7 percent to -0.1 percent, thereby reducing a substantial portion of the excessive optimism prevailing in the market.

The imposition of regulatory constraints has implications for fairness and efficiency. Suppose that every investor's allocation in the constrained equilibrium features higher expected utility than in the unconstrained equilibrium (when both are measured with respect to the correct probability vector Π). Does this mean that the imposition of regulatory constraints has resulted in an increase in fairness coupled with a loss in efficiency? That depends on both the definitions of fairness and efficiency.

Constraining investors to act as if they are smarter, or less vulnerable to emotion, might improve fairness defined in terms of freedom from misrepresentation, equal information, equal processing ability, freedom from impulse, and equal bargaining power. However, by their nature constraints involve coercion, thereby leading to reduced fairness defined as freedom from coercion.

As to efficiency, forcing investors to trade as if they hold beliefs $\{Q_i\}$ which are different from $\{P_i\}$ moves the equilibrium allocation off the Pareto-efficiency frontier defined by $\{P_i\}$, but onto the Pareto-efficiency frontier defined by $\{Q_i\}$. Hence, when investors view markets through the lens of $\{P_i\}$, they perceive that the constraints result in a move off the Pareto-efficient frontier. However, efficiency can also be defined as informational efficiency. If regulatory constraints lead the representative investor to hold beliefs in the Q-equilibrium which are closer to Π than in the P-equilibrium, regulations might lead to an improvement in efficiency defined relative to correct prices. By definition, such a situation would also be viewed as an increase in fairness, when fairness is defined as the right to trade at correct prices.

7.2 Biased Cost–Benefit Assessment

Hirshleifer (2008b) focuses attention on the manner in which systematic biases on the part of participants in the political process impact regulatory outcomes. He calls his framework the psychological attraction approach to regulation, because particular parties advocating increased regulation exploit psychological biases to attract attention and support. The basis for Hirshleifer's framework is the following series of seven phenomena.

1. Salience and vividness effects: Regulatory debates are influenced heavily by extreme events, and by heart-rending personal stories. Hirshleifer points out that accounting scandals such as occurred at firms such as Enron and WorldCom precipitated passage of the Sarbanes–Oxley Act of 2002 (or SOX). He points out that the costs of disclosure imposed by SOX are less vivid than poignant stories about families who suffered large losses.[2] He suggests that the focus on individual

[2] The constitutionality of SOX is currently before the U.S. Supreme Court, which will rule on the issue in 2010.

losses is amplified through conversation and media reporting, which are biased toward the communication of adverse and emotionally charged news. This tendency applies to losses suffered from derivatives trading, thereby leading the public to attach negative perceptions of derivatives. As a result, the public tends to overlook benefits associated with derivatives, such as hedging, leading to a disposition to regulate derivatives.

2. Omission bias: This bias involves the favoring of omissions over commissions. As an example, regulation intended to protect unsophisticated investors from securities lacking merit might also prevent them from risk-reducing diversification.
3. Scapegoating and xenophobia: When things go wrong, people instinctively seek someone to blame, such as members of a visible, disliked, and relatively weak out-group. Economic and stock market downturns increase pressure for regulation targeting specific culprits. Hirshleifer cites the Securities Acts of 1933 and 1934, and the Sarbanes–Oxley Act as examples.
4. Fairness and reciprocity norms: Hirshleifer's view of fairness partly overlaps with the discussion above. He focuses on three norms, namely reciprocity, equality, and charity. Reciprocity involves quid pro quo. Equality involves equal division of resources. Charity involves acts intended to relieve distress. According to Hirshleifer, reciprocity motivates scapegoating, particularly as intermediaries are seen by the public as adding little value. Equality underlies hostility to lenders, a view underlying regulations to prevent usury. Charity is directed at addressing recent losses. Considerations of fairness can explain regulations intended to limit speculation, restrict short-selling, and penalize short-term capital gains.
5. Overconfidence: According to Hirshleifer, overconfidence helps to explain the existence of excessive regulation. He cites the work of Adam Smith and Friedrich Hayek in respect to a spontaneous order, understood as a web of coadaptations resulting from individual decisions, that is too complex for a central planner to comprehend. Hirshleifer asserts that

overconfidence leads public officials to believe that they can institute regulatory mechanisms which can improve on market allocation. As examples, he mentions transactions taxes to limit speculation and monetary policy to address irrationally exuberant equity markets or to provide stimulus during an economic downturn. He suggests that the better-than-average effect induces encourages regulators to believe they are more skilled than investors at identifying the value of the market. He suggests that the illusion of control leads regulators to conclude that they are able to avert bubbles and crashes. In this last regard, he indicates that following adverse outcomes, regulators come under criticism for failing to prevent unfavorable outcome, which leads to calls for more strict regulation.

6. Mood effects and availability cascades: Hirshleifer makes the point that short-term moods impact judgments and decisions relating to the long-term. Moreover, mood can be contagious, thereby aggregating at the social level. In this respect, the call for greater regulation by a few can lead others to infer that there is good reason to do so. Information cascades can develop, whereby the increased social discourse about an issue leads to the perception that the issue is truly important.
7. Ideological replicators: Ideologies, be they religious, political, or economic, shape financial regulation through word of mouth. Hirshleifer suggests that conspiracy theories are prone to develop during market crashes. He makes the point that the general public have a poor understanding of how major players in financial markets affect risks. In this regard, he singles out hedge fund managers as being especially suspect, as they operate in secrecy, and are often foreigners.

7.3 Regulation and Financial Crises

Elizabeth Warren is a member of Harvard University Law faculty who specializes in bankruptcy. Currently, she also heads the committee which oversees the dispensing of funds from the Troubled Assets

Relief Plan (TARP) passed by Congress in 2008 to rescue key financial institutions in distress. In Rather (2009), Warren reminds us of some history, that a financial crisis including a credit squeeze accompanied the 1792 crisis, the first economic crisis in U.S. history. Major financial crises occurred every 15–20 years between 1792 and 1929. As Shefrin and Statman (2009) point out, the stock market crash of 1929 and Great Depression following heated regulatory irons to extremely high temperatures, facilitating strikes that changed their shapes radically, including the Securities Act of 1933, the Securities Exchange Act of 1934, and the Glass-Steagall Act which separated commercial and investment banking.

Warren pointed out that no major financial crises occurred between 1934 and the 1980s that were comparable in scale to those occurring before the Great Depression. However, since 1980, a process of deregulation has been underway, which she notes has been accompanied by two major financial crises in the United States, the savings and loan (S&L) crisis of the 1980s, and the financial crisis in 2008–2009.

The parallels between the S&L crisis of the 1980s and the financial crisis of 2008–2009 are striking, and strongly suggests the collective failure to learn. For both crises, the key features involved the following:

- the market for real estate;
- a political and regulatory environment encouraging home ownership;
- fixed income securities at the core of the crisis;
- a period of interest rate volatility featuring low real interest rates followed by high real interest rates;
- S&L institutions as key players;
- a period of active deregulation featuring low capital ratios;
- risk-seeking behavior by financial institutions;
- subprime loans, featuring acquisition, development, and construction loans in the S&L crisis, and subprime mortgages in the 2008–2009 crisis;
- the funding of projects with a high probability of generating poor cash flows;

— agency issues on the part of real estate appraisers in the S&L crisis and rating firms in the financial crisis of 2008–2009;
— high accounting profits reported by financial institutions;
— large bonuses to executives;
— pyramid (Ponzi) schemes;
— government agencies becoming insolvent: the FSLIC insuring S&Ls becoming insolvent in 1987, and in 2009 the FDIC was nearing insolvency; and
— subsequent turbulence in equity markets.

In the discussion below I highlight some of the parallels in the above list, first by describing the S&L crisis, and then the financial crisis of 2008–2009.

7.3.1 S&L Crisis in the 1980s

Until the 1980s, regulations restricted S&Ls to deposits and home mortgage loans. Notably, interest rate ceilings prevented S&Ls from paying competitive interest rates on deposits. During the late 1970s, when the critical seeds of the S&L crisis were sown, nominal capital requirements were low (6 percent of liabilities). Because of inflation, nominal interest rates rose dramatically at this time, leading to an outflow of deposits from S&Ls. For the industry as a whole, these increases caused the market value of their assets to fall below the market value of their liabilities. However, there was no fair value accounting in place at the time, and so this state of affairs was not recognized within the industry's financial statements.

The industry response to the changing economic environment featured status quo bias. Essentially the industry continued to hold mortgages it originated, but did not

— lengthen term of its deposits,
— hedge its risk exposures,
— shorten the term of its mortgages, and
— sell mortgages and buy shorter term assets.

Regulatory reform began to take shape in the period 1980–1982. Legislators granted the S&L industry the power to enter new areas of business, intended to increase S&L profits as opposed to promoting housing and homeownership. For example, the Depository Institutions Deregulation and Monetary Control Act (DIDMCA) made the following changes:

- — removed interest rate ceiling on deposit accounts,
- — expanded authority for federal S&Ls to make ADC loans, and
- — raised the deposit insurance limit raised to $100,000 from $40,000.

The Garn-St. Germain Act of 1982 was a Reagan administration initiative for federally chartered S&Ls. It eliminated previous statutory limit on the loan to value ratio, and permitted the portfolios of these S&Ls to comprise up to

- — 40 percent of assets in commercial mortgages,
- — 30 percent of assets in consumer loans,
- — 10 percent of assets in commercial loans, and
- — 10 percent of assets in commercial leases.

At the same time that regulatory restrictions on the S&L industry were being lifted, the ability of regulatory authorities to monitor the industry was reduced. The Federal Home Loan Bank Board was the agency responsible for regulating S&Ls. Between 1980 and 1985 Bank Board

- — reduced net worth requirements for insured S&L institutions,
- — removed limits on the amounts of brokered deposits an S&L could hold,
- — permitted lax accounting standards, and
- — reduced the size of its regulatory and supervisory staff.

During the early 1980s, most S&Ls were reporting losses. Garn-St. Germain and DIDMCA increased S&L's risk-seeking opportunities for funding high risk development projects. Many institutions took advantage of these opportunities, in what might have featured aversion to a sure loss, but definitely featured fraud. For those readers who instinctively hold a *laissez faîre* philosophy and believe in market efficiency, should find the following value destructive sequence of events instructive.

Value destroying S&Ls seized newfound opportunities in the market for commercial property loans, by granting loans to developers of low-quality projects for amounts that overstated the value of these projects. In doing so, the S&Ls communicated the size of the proposed loan to potential appraisers, asking for preliminary appraisals. S&Ls then selected high appraisers and rewarded them with a continuing stream of business. The same phenomenon manifested itself 20 years later with ratings firms. Notably, these large loans featured an "anticipated profit component," reflecting the inflated values of their projects.

The loans just described were for interest only, with principal due in two-to-three years. Notably, the terms of these loans held back the interest payments due, and these payments were subsequently booked as income on S&Ls' financial statements, along with points and fees. S&Ls preferred weak developers, as they would agree to high interest rates.

For those readers who believe the discipline of the market will surely curtail such behavior, read on. To be sure, at some point it would become apparent and did, especially to the S&Ls, that the cash flows from most of these low quality, high risk projects, were low. Could the S&Ls avoid recognizing the losses in question? Yes, if they could find buyers for these projects, which they did, in a scheme called "cash for trash." The scheme involved locating other weak developers searching for loans, who agreed to purchase the failing projects of others at inflated prices, together with a profit sharing arrangement. The inflated prices in "cash for trash" resulted in book profits for these projects, and the S&Ls extracted a 50–50 profit split. Being market transactions, the associated gains were registered as income on these S&Ls' financial statements. This made the firms appear to be profitable, induced clean opinions by auditors, and attracted more depositors, who would be protected by higher deposit insurance limits. See Black (2005).

Eventually, this pyramid scheme would have to end, and the S&L would fail. However, that does not mean that the S&L executives would fail. Indeed, executives would have paid themselves substantial bonuses for having turned around a nearly failed bank at a time when the whole industry was in decline. Perhaps, they were sufficiently overconfident to believe that their fraudulent behavior would go undetected.

In 1983, the Bank Board came under new leadership, with the appointment of Ed Gray. Gray made a strong effort to reverse the direction of deregulation, and to recapitalize the FSLIC, which was in the process of going insolvent. His attempts to investigate one particular S&L, Lincoln Savings and Loan, led him to be summoned by five Senators who questioned the appropriateness of his actions. In the end, Lincoln's failure cost U.S. taxpayers over \$2 billion. The total cost of addressing the failures in the S&L industry was approximately \$150 Billion.

7.3.2 Financial Crisis of 2008–2009

Opinions about the root cause of the financial crisis of 2008–2009 differ. Posner (2009) argues that the root lies with a weak regulatory structure, within which private-sector decisions were largely rational. Akerlof and Shiller (2009) argue that the root lies with irrational decisions associated with the occurrence of a housing market bubble, a surge in subprime mortgage lending, and the breakdown of the rational adverse selection ("lemons") paradigm. Brunnermeier et al. (2008) and Taylor (2009) also argue that an asset pricing bubble was a major issue, which they trace to low U.S. interest rates during the period 2003–2006. Sullivan (2009) blames poor corporate governance, explicit corruption, and unwise governmental mandates and guarantees. Differentiating among these various views requires a search for the devil in the details.

In Shefrin (2009), I suggest that each of the above explanations contains an element of truth. The regulatory structure was weak, interest rates were low, there was a housing market bubble, the surge in subprime mortgage lending was highly problematic, and there were failures in governance at financial firms.

One lesson not learned from the S&L crisis involves failing to recognize the dangers from simultaneously expanding risky alternatives to financial institutions and reducing regulatory oversight, if not ignoring the warnings from regulators. In this regard, the Gramm–Leach–Bliley

Act of 1999 fragmented regulatory oversight so that no regulator had a comprehensive picture of each financial firm. The Commodity Futures Modernization Act left the derivatives market without regulatory oversight. This occurred despite the warnings issued by the head of the Commodity Futures Trading Commission, Brooksley Born, who was subsequently relieved of her position for issuing those warnings. See PBS (2009) which documents Born's concerns, and the opposition to it from Federal Reserve Chair Alan Greenspan, and Clinton administration officials Robert Rubin and Larry Summers.

Another regulator whose warnings went in vain was Comptroller of the Currency John Dugan (CNN, 2008). In mid-2005, he was among the first to sound the alarm about risky lending in the housing market, saying that many buyers, particularly those with bad credit, would soon be unable to afford their mortgage payments. He added that if housing prices declined, homeowners would be unable to sell their homes, and foreclosure rates would rise dramatically.

During 2005, bank regulators observed deteriorating conditions in the mortgage market, and proposed new guidelines for banks writing risky loans. In line with capture theory, the banking industry lobbied against the proposal. The governments banking agencies spent nearly a year debating the rules, which required unanimous agreement among different regulatory bodies, including the Federal Reserve. The industry succeeded in achieving a one-year delay, with new rules released in late 2006, and the strictest of the proposed provisions gone. The provisions stripped from the final rules included the following:

— Banks that bundle and sell mortgages must disclose to investors exactly what they are buying;
— Banks must advise home buyers that interest rates might increase dramatically, resulting in payments becoming due sooner than expected;
— Banks must verify that buyers actually have jobs and can afford houses; and
— Banks must cap their risky mortgages so that a string of defaults would not be crippling.

Consider the comments of Alan Greenspan, who chaired the Federal Reserve during the key years in which the seeds of the crisis were sown. In June 2005, Greenspan testified before Congress that some local housing markets exhibited "froth." He pointed to the use of risky financing by some homeowners and suggested that the price increases in those local markets were unsustainable. However, he concluded that there was no national housing bubble and that the economy was not at risk. In the same vein, Greenspan's successor at the Fed, Ben Bernanke, gave a speech on 17 May 2007 in which he stated, "[W]e do not expect significant spillovers from the subprime market to the rest of the economy or to the financial system."

In 2008, Greenspan testified before the House of Representatives Committee on Oversight and Government Reform. Below is an excerpt from his appearance, beginning with a question from committee chair Henry Waxman.

> Henry Waxman: You were the longest serving chairman of the Federal Reserve in history and during this period of time were perhaps the leading proponent of deregulation of our financial markets. Certainly you were the most influential voice for deregulation. You have been a staunch advocate for letting markets regulate themselves. ... My question for you is simple, were you wrong?
>
> Alan Greenspan: I made a mistake in presuming that the self-interest of organizations, specifically banks and others, was capable of protecting their own shareholders and the equity in the firms, and it has been my experience, having worked both as a regulator for 18 years and similar quantities in the private sector, especially 10 years at a major international bank, that the loan officers of those institutions knew far more about the risks involved and the people to whom they lent money than I saw even our best regulators at the fed capable of doing. So the problem here is something which looked

> to be a very solid edifice and indeed a critical pillar to market competition and free markets did break down and I think that shocked me. I still do not fully understand why it happened and obviously to the extent that I figure out where it happened and why, I will change my views. …
>
> Henry Waxman: This is your statement. "I do have an ideology. My judgment is that free competitive markets are by far the unrivaled way to organize economies. We have tried regulation, none meaningfully worked." That was your quote. You had the authority to prevent irresponsible lending practices that led to the subprime mortgage crisis. You were advised to do so by many others. And now our whole economy is paying its price. Do you feel that your ideology pushed you to make decisions that you wish you had not made?
>
> Alan Greenspan: I found a flaw in the model that I perceived as the critical functioning structure that defines how the world works. … [T]his crisis, however, has turned out to be much broader than anything I could have imagined ⋯ Those of us who have looked to the self-interest of lending institutions to protect shareholders' equity-myself especially-are in a state of shocked disbelief.

I suggest that the flaw in Greenspan's model, and the missing pieces in his understanding of what happened, lies in behavioral finance. In this regard, psychological issues such as overconfidence, excessive optimism, confirmation bias, and aversion to a sure loss played major roles in the decision processes at investment banks, rating agencies, insurance firms, institutional investors, and regulatory agencies.

In Shefrin (2009), I present a series of case studies demonstrating that the financial crisis of 2008–2009 was driven by a combination of sentiment in asset prices and organizational issues that are at the heart of behavioral corporate finance. The case studies highlight (to a greater or lesser degree) irrational decision making at key points in the financial product supply chain. I emphasize that psychological pitfalls dominated the key processes at financial firms. As mentioned in Shefrin (2009), these processes pertained to goal setting, planning, incentives, and information sharing. Below are highlights from the cases, all of which highlight the importance of debiasing.

AIG

American International Group (AIG) is an insurance firm which facilitated the explosive growth in subprime mortgage lending in 2004 and 2005 by selling credit default spreads (CDS) that insured against default. AIG's financial product division irrationally failed to track the proportion of subprime mortgages in the pools being insured, thereby misgauging the risk of those assets and causing the associated CDS contracts to be mispriced. Interestingly, this failure occurred despite employee incentives that balanced long-term performance against short-term performance. Moreover, conversations that AIG had with its investment bank trading partners indicate the presence of a widespread conservatism bias regarding the assumption that historical mortgage default rates would continue to apply.

In 2004 and 2005, the activities of financial institutions might have been rational because they were able to shift default risk to AIG by purchasing credit default swap protection. However, after AIG stopped selling CDS contracts, many financial firms took on the risk themselves, apparently under the illusion that housing prices would continue to rise and that default rates would not be affected by the increased ratio of subprime to prime mortgages. At one point, Merrill Lynch used CDS contracts to create synthetic collateralized debt obligations (CDOs) because the number of subprime mortgages available to create traditional CDOs was insufficient relative to the firm's aspirations.

UBS

UBS's investment banking division admitted to misgauging subprime mortgage risk by not "looking through" the CDO structures and by assuming that historical default rates would continue to apply. UBS's underperformance relative to competitors led them to exhibit reference point-induced risk seeking. This behavior was compounded by poor incentive structures at UBS that emphasized short-term performance over long-term performance.

UBS placed no operational limits on the size of its CDO warehouse. It was not alone. Investment banks are typically intermediaries, not end investors planning to hold large positions in subprime mortgages. Some hold the equity tranches of CDOs as a signal to the buyers of the less risky tranches. What created many of the losses for investment banks, however, was inventory risk–risk stemming from warehousing the subprime positions that underlay CDOs. As the housing market fell into decline, many investment banks found that they could not locate buyers for the CDOs and, as a result, inadvertently became end investors.

Rating Agencies: S&P and Moody's

The rating agencies and investors' reliance on them played a huge role in the financial crisis. Both (supposedly) sophisticated investors, such as the investment bankers at UBS, and naive end investors, relied on the risk assessments of rating agencies. However, the rating agencies explicitly indicated that their ratings were premised on accepting the information they received as accurate, even if the mortgages featured limited documentation. For this reason, these agencies suggested that their ratings be treated as only one piece of information when assessing risk. By this argument, users who accepted their ratings at face value behaved irrationally.

Did the rating agencies exhibit irrational behavior by weakening their risk assessment criteria to cultivate more business? This question is different from asking whether the ratings agencies behaved ethically. The major problem with the behavior of rating agencies might arise more from a conflict of interests (the principal–agent conflict) than irrationality, in the sense that the issuers of securities, not the end investors in the securities, pay for ratings. At the same time, I suggest that reference point-induced risk seeking and groupthink played major roles at rating agency S&P.

In this regard, Griffin and Tang (2009) find that ratings by Moody's and S&P were higher than what their models implied. They conclude that tranches that were rated AAA actually corresponded to BBB when rated according to the firms' models and default standards.

SEC

The SEC came under intense criticism for its lax oversight of investment banking practices and for failing to detect a large hedge fund Ponzi scheme run by Bernard Madoff. A focal point of the criticism of investment bank oversight involved a meeting that took place at the SEC on April 28, 2004, when the commission was chaired by William Donaldson. That meeting established the Consolidated Supervised Entities (CSE) program, a voluntary regulatory program that allowed the SEC to review the capital structure and risk management procedures of participating financial institutions. Five investment banks joined the CSE program, as did two bank holding companies. The investment banks were Bear Stearns, Goldman Sachs, Lehman Brothers, Merrill Lynch, and Morgan Stanley, and the bank holding companies were Citigroup and JPMorgan Chase. Subsequent to the April 2004 meeting, the SEC failed to provide qualified staff in sufficient numbers to effectively monitor these financial institutions.

As to the Bernard Madoff Ponzi scheme, the largest in history, the SEC issued an internal report in the summer of 2009. The report indicates that between 1992 and 2008, the agency received six distinct complaints about Madoff's operations, one of which involved three separate versions. Several of the complaints suggested that Madoff was running a Ponzi scheme. The report reveals that the SEC conducted investigations and examinations related to Madoff's investment advisory business but failed to uncover the fraud, largely because it ignored pertinent evidence that it uncovered. I suggest that confirmation bias lay at the heart of the SEC's failure to detect Madoff's Ponzi scheme.

Regulatory Response

In June 2009, President Obama proposed a broad new regulatory framework for financial markets, emphasizing a centralized structure for oversight, with the Federal Reserve Bank playing a central role. Among the other proposals is the creation of a consumer protection agency, suggested by Elizabeth Warren. Notably, there is opposition to this last proposal from the financial services industry. The SEC's Division of Enforcement Management is in the process of developing a plan to restructure its approach through five new specialized units. These units would focus on investment companies (including hedge funds and private equity firms), market abuses, complex derivatives, the municipal securities market, and bribery issues in foreign countries involving U.S. companies.

In October 2009, the House Financial Services Committee voted to pass the "Accountability and Transparency in Rating Agencies Act" in order to address some of the issues mentioned above. This Act allows investors to sue rating agencies for knowingly or recklessly failing to review key information in their ratings, provides the SEC with authority to sanction supervisors at credit rating agencies for failing to supervise employees, and contains requirements to mitigate the conflicts of interest that result because it is the issuers who actually pay rating agencies, not the investors.

7.3.3 Market Prices

Figure 7.1 displays the monthly time series of stock prices between 1984 and 2009. As can be seen, both the period associated with the S&L crisis and the financial crisis of 2008–2009 featured considerable turbulence. The stock market crash of October 1987 occurred in the midst of the S&L crisis.

Figure 7.2 displays an update of the analysis in Shiller (1981, 2005). The point Shiller makes in this figure is that market prices are excessively volatile relative to dividends. In making this point, he uses three different discount rates. Two discount rates are time varying and are derived from aggregate consumption and market interest rates, respectively. The third discount rate is time invariant.

Notice from Figure 7.2 that after 1991, market prices exceeded intrinsic value no matter which of the three proxies for intrinsic value is used. According to this figure, the financial crisis of 2008–2009 merely

Fig. 7.1 Display of the monthly time series of stock prices between 1984 and 2009. *Source*: Shiller (2005) and http://www.irrationalexuberance.com/index.htm.

served to bring stock prices into alignment with fundamental value. The data displayed in Figure 7.2 are annual, with the 2009 value corresponding to June. Stock prices were approximately 18 percent lower at the trough in March, and ended 2009 20 percent higher than in June. Given that Shiller's measures for intrinsic value move much more slowly than market prices, one might infer that the market was 20 percent undervalued at the trough in March, but moved to become 20 percent overvalued by year end.

Shiller bases his measures for intrinsic value on aggregate dividend flows. However, Boudoukh et al. (2007) analyze how intrinsic values for stocks should reflect the present value of future payouts, not just dividends. Payouts include share repurchases. Their analysis suggests that as the ratio of dividends to payouts declined after the 1970s, Shiller's measures might have become biased downward. This might explain why stock prices continued well above intrinsic value, even after the collapse of the dot-com bubble.

A final point to note is that along the decomposition of total returns along the intrinsic value paths features a much larger contribution from

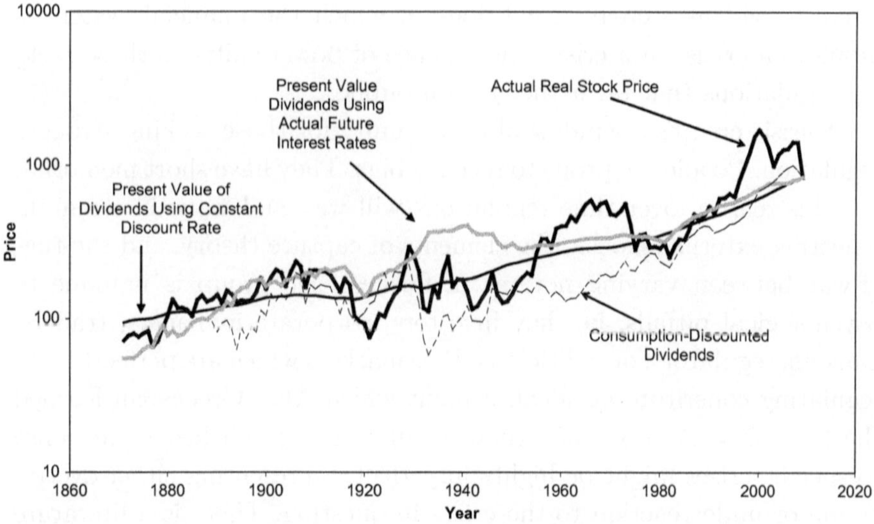

Fig. 7.2 Comparing actual real stock price with three alternative PDVs of future real dividends. *Source*: Shiller (2005) and http://www.irrationalexuberance.com/index.htm.

dividend yield than is the case with market value. With market value, the lion's share of total return stems from stock price appreciation, not dividend yield. However, for the measure of intrinsic value associated with the time invariant discount rate, price changes are very gradual, thereby forcing most of the return to be generated by the dividend yield.

7.4 Differences in Perspective

Hirshleifer's perspective emphasizes overregulation, stemming from the psychological underweighting of regulatory costs relative to benefits. In many ways, his position is similar to the general position that guided Alan Greenspan's approach to regulation when he chaired the Federal Reserve.

On the other hand, capture theory suggests that private interests will seek to exploit the regulatory framework to their advantage, relative to the general public. Much of the time, their efforts will succeed, and they will achieve greater power than those seeking stronger regulation that favors the general public. However, the efforts of special interests will also create conditions in which the financial system is prone to a crisis. In a crisis, the balance of power shifts to those seeking regulations that favor the general public.

A crisis creates a window of opportunity for those seeking stronger regulation. People are prone to recency bias. They have short memories. For this reason, over time regulations will wax and wane in strength, reflecting external shocks, the elements of capture theory, and the tug-of-war between varying notions of fairness. No group is immune to psychological pitfalls, be they investors, corporate managers, traders, bankers, regulators, or politicians. Free markets which are perfectly self-regulating constitute an ideal, a point which Alan Greenspan learned the hard way. At the same time, regulations established in response to specific crises might be highly imperfect, representing either overreaction or underreaction to the crises in question. There is a literature suggesting that some of the provisions in the Sarbanes–Oxley Act are in this vein. Regulatory agencies are imperfect, as the discussion about the SEC demonstrates. It is easy to have debates about regulation on broad principles. However, any serious discussion of financial market regulation needs to highlight behavioral biases and be based on facts rather than ideology.

8

Concluding Remarks

Behavioral finance is in the process of transforming the financial paradigm from a neoclassical framework to a framework that explicitly incorporates psychological phenomena. In this monograph I describe highlights of the behavioral finance literature, focusing attention on both its strengths and its weaknesses.

Behavioral finance has brought a realistic dimension to finance, replacing unrealistic assumptions neoclassical finance makes about investors and managers being fully rational and market prices being efficient. At the same time, a significant portion of the behavioral finance literature lacks rigor, and indeed some of its claims appear to be in error. In addition to surveying the foundations underlying the behavioral literature, I use this monograph to identify trends — possible future directions for behavioral finance. I suggest that the future of academic finance will combine the realism offered by behavioral finance with the rigor offered by neoclassical finance. Sections 4 through 7 of this monograph provide some specific ideas for what shape the behavioralization of finance might take.

The approach to behavioral preferences begins with the behavior that motivated prospect theory: gains and losses relative to a reference point as carriers of value, the four-fold pattern for risk attitudes, psychophysics, and editing. Notably, prospect theory ignores the role of emotion in decision making. In addition, its formalization possesses some structural weaknesses. For these reasons, behavioral preferences will add features in other psychological-based theories of risk such as regret, self-control, and the emotions emphasized in SP/A theory. My view of behavioral beliefs is that they are best modeled as imperfect learning systems that are heuristic-driven and violate Bayes' rule. Formally, it will be convenient to represent behavioral beliefs using change of measure techniques, especially for studying the impact of beliefs on asset pricing.

Behavioral beliefs and preferences serve as the basis for behavioralizing portfolio theory. Behavioral portfolios are structured to satisfy a variety of financial and psychological needs. Behavioral portfolios reflect a series of psychological phenomena such as status quo bias, the attention hypothesis, the disposition effect, overconfidence, and the predilection for lottery stocks, cash dividends, structured products, and covered call option positions. Behavioral portfolios tend to be undiversified. In the future, behavioral portfolio models will feature combined diffusion/jump processes to capture the tendency of investors to make adjustments to their portfolios intermittently rather than continuously in time. These models will feature the combination of status quo bias and other psychological traits.

The behavioralization of asset pricing theory will replace unrealistic neoclassical assumptions with more realistic psychologically based assumptions in models built around the SDF. In this regard, systematic risk will feature both fundamentals and sentiment. Sentiment will be expressed as a log-change of measure. Risk premiums will be determined through the SDF and mean-variance (MV) frontier in analogous ways to neoclassical theory, except that the SDF and MV-frontier will reflect sentiment. Behavioral asset pricing models have already begun to generalize neoclassical asset pricing models, especially for the term structure of interest rates and option prices. In addition, work on identifying return anomalies will continue. A recent example pertains to the U.S. Presidential election cycle. See Kräussl et al. (2009).

Some of the most recent behavioral advances have occurred in corporate finance. I focus attention on three areas that strike me as especially germane to future contributions. They are: (1) the influence of corporate managers' personal characteristics on their corporate decisions; (2) the impact of social networks on corporate decisions and corporate value; and (3) the psychological profiles of entrepreneurs.

At present there is but a small literature in financial market regulation, which might explain why financial economists were ill equipped to comment on the aftermath of the financial crisis of 2008–2009. It seems to me that psychological pitfalls lie at the heart of the financial crisis of 2008–2009, and for this reason it will be important going forward for financial economists to study the role of psychology in financial market regulation. I suggest that by and large, the lessons of the S&L crisis of the 1980s largely went unheeded, and the seeds of that crisis were allowed to germinate and wreck havoc two decades later.

If there is a lesson in this monograph for economists, it is this. Going forward, neoclassical economists need to incorporate more psychology into their models, and behavioral economists need to incorporate more rigor into theirs. The future lies with both groups meeting in the middle.

References

Aït-Sahalia, Y. and A. Lo (2000), 'Nonparametric risk management and implied risk aversion'. *Journal of Econometrics* **94**, 9–51.

Akerlof, G. and R. Shiller (2009), *Animal Spirits: How Human Psychology Drives the Economy, and Why it Matters for Global Capitalism.* Princeton, NJ: Princeton University Press.

Allais, M. (1953), 'La psychologie de l'hômme rationnel devant le risque: critique des postulats et axiomes de l' école américaine'. *Econometrica* **21**, 503–546.

Allport, G. W. and L. J. Postman (1947), *The Psychology of Rumor.* Holt, New York.

Anderson, T. W. (1932), *Remembering: A Study in Experimental and Social Psychology.* London York: Cambridge University Press.

Andreassen, P. B. and S. J. Kraus (1990), 'Judgemental extrapolation and the salience of change'. *Journal of Forecasting* **9**, 347–372.

Ang, J. and Y. Cheng (2009), 'Direct evidence on the market-driven acquisitions theory'. *Journal of Financial Research,* forthcoming.

Arkes, H., L. Herren, and A. Isen (1988), 'The role of potential loss in the influence of affect on risk-taking behavior'. *Organizational Behavior and Human Decision Processes* **66**, 228–236.

Asch, S. (1956), 'Studies of independence and conformity: A minority of one against a unanimous majority'. *Psychological Monographs* **70**, Whole No. 416.

Baker, M., J. Coval, and J. Stein (2004), 'Corporate financing decisions when investors take the path of least resistance'. *Journal of Financial Economics* **84**, 266–298.

Baker, M., S. Nagel, and J. Wurgler (2007a), 'The Effect of Dividends on Consumption'. *Brookings Papers on Economic Activity* pp. 277–291.

Baker, M., R. Ruback, and J. Wurgler (2007b), 'Behavioral corporate finance: A survey'. In: E. Eckbo (ed.): *The Handbook of Corporate Finance: Empirical Corporate Finance*. New York: Elsevier/North Holland.

Baker, M., J. Stein, and J. Wurgler (2003), 'When does the market matter? Stock prices and the investment of equity-dependent firms'. *Quarterly Journal of Economics* **118**, 969–1006.

Baker, M. and J. C. Stein (2004), 'Market liquidity as a sentiment indicator'. *Journal of Financial Markets* **7**, 271–99.

Baker, M. and J. Wurgler (2002), 'Market timing and capital structure'. *Journal of Finance* **57**, 1–32.

Baker, M. and J. Wurgler (2004a), 'Appearing and disappearing dividends: The link to catering incentives'. *Journal of Financial Economics* **73**, 271–288.

Baker, M. and J. Wurgler (2004b), 'A catering theory of dividends'. *Journal of Finance* **59**, 271–288.

Baker, M. and J. Wurgler (2006), 'Investor sentiment and the cross-section of stock returns'. *Journal of Finance* **61**, 1645–1680.

Baker, M. and J. Wurgler (2007), 'Investor sentiment in the stock market'. *Journal of Economics Perspectives* **21**, 129–151.

Bakshi, G. S., C. Cao, and Z. Chen (2000), 'Do call prices and the underlying stock always move in the same direction'. *Review of Financial Studies* **13**, 549–584.

Balduzzi, P., D. Das, and S. Foresi (1998), 'The central tendency: a second factor in bond yields'. *Review of Economics and Statistics* **80**, 62–72.

Barber, B., Y. Lee, Y. Liu, and T. Odean (2005), 'Do individual day traders make money? Evidence from Taiwan'. Working Paper, University of California, Davis.

Barber, B., Y. Lee, Y. Liu, and T. Odean (2009a), 'Just how much do individual investors lose by trading?'. *Review of Financial Studies* **22**, 609–632.

Barber, B. and T. Odean (2000), 'Trading is hazardous to your wealth: The common stock performance of individual investors'. *Journal of Finance* **55**, 773–806.

Barber, B. and T. Odean (2008), 'All that glitters: The effect of attention on the buying behavior of individual and institutional investors'. *Review of Financial Studies* **21**, 785–818.

Barber, B., T. Odean, and N. Zhu (2009b), 'Do retail trades move markets'. *Review of Financial Studies* **22**, 151–186.

Barberis, N. and M. Huang (2001), 'Mental accounting, loss aversion and individual stock returns'. *Journal of Finance* **56**, 1247–1292.

Barberis, N. and M. Huang (2008), 'Stocks as lotteries: The implications of probability weighting for security prices'. *American Economic Review* **98**, 2066–2100.

Barberis, N., M. Huang, and T. Santos (2001a), 'Prospect theory and asset prices'. *Quarterly Journal of Economics* **116**, 1–53.

Barberis, N. and A. Shleifer (2003), 'Style investing'. *Journal of Financial Economics* **68**, 161–199.

Barberis, N., A. Shleifer, and R. Vishny (1998), 'A model of investor sentiment'. *Journal of Financial Economics* **49**, 307–345.

Barberis, N., A. Shleifer, and J. Wurgler (2001b), 'Comovement'. Working Paper, University of Chicago.

Barberis, N. and R. Thaler (2003), 'A Survey of behavioral finance'. In: G. Constantinides, R. Stulz, and M. Harris (eds.): *Handbook of the Economics of Finance*. North Holland.

Barberis, N. and W. Xiong (2009), 'What drives the disposition effect? An analysis of a long-standing preference-based explanation'. *Journal of Finance* **64**, 751–784.

Barone-Adesi, G., R. Engle, and L. Mancini (2008), 'A GARCH option pricing model with filtered historical simulation'. *Review of Financial Studies* **21**, 1223–1258.

Barone-Adesi, G., P. Gagliardini, and G. Urga (2004), 'Testing asset pricing models with coskewness'. *Journal of Business & Economic Statistics* **22**, 474–485.

Barone-Adesi, G. and P. Talwar (1983), 'Market models and heteroscedasticity of residual security returns'. *Journal of Business & Economic Statistics* **1**, 163–168.

Barsky, R. B., M. S. Kimball, F. T. Juster, and M. D. Shapiro (1997), 'Preference parameters and behavioral heterogeneity: An experimental approach in the health and retirement survey'. *Quarterly Journal of Economics* **112**, 537–579.

Ben-David, I., J. Graham, and C. Harvey (2007), 'Managerial overconfidence and corporate policies'. Working paper, Duke University.

Bénabou, R. (2008), 'Groupthink: Collective delusions in organizations and markets'. Working Paper, Princeton University.

Benartzi, S. (2001), 'Excessive extrapolation and the allocation of 401(k) accounts to company stock'. *Journal of Finance* **56**, 1747–1764.

Benartzi, S., E. Peleg, and R. Thaler (2009), 'Choice architecture and retirement saving plans'. In: E. Shafir (ed.): *The Behavioral Foundations of Policy.* Russell Sage Foundation and Princeton University Press, forthcoming.

Benartzi, S. and R. Thaler (1995), 'Myopic loss aversion and the equity premium puzzle'. *Quarterly Journal of Economics* pp. 73–92.

Benartzi, S. and R. Thaler (2001), 'Nave diversification strategies in defined contribution savings plans'. *American Economic Review* **91**, 79–98.

Benartzi, S. and R. Thaler (2007), 'Heuristics and biases in retirement savings behavior'. *Journal of Economic Perspectives* **21**, 81–104.

Bergstresser, D., M. Desai, and J. Rauh (2004), 'Earnings manipulation and managerial investment decisions: Evidence from sponsored pension plans'. *Quarterly Journal of Economics* **121**, 157–195.

Bernard, C. and P. Boyle (2008), 'Structured investment products with caps and floors'. Working paper, University of Waterloo.

Bitler, M., T. Moskowitz, and A. Vissing-Jorgensen (2004), 'Testing agency theory with entrepreneur effort and wealth'. *Journal of Finance* **60**, 539–576.

Black, W. (2005), 'Control fraud as an explanation for white-collar crime waves: The case of the savings & loan debacle'. *Crime, Law and Social Change* **43**, 1–29.

Blackburn, D. and A. Ukhov (2006), 'Estimating preferences toward risk: Evidence from Dow Jones'. Working Paper, University of Indiana.

Blume, L. and D. Easley (2008), 'Market selection and asset pricing'. In: T. Hens and K. Schenk-Hoppé (eds.): *Handbook of Financial Markets: Dynamics and Evolution*. Amsterdam: Elsevier.

Boudoukh, J., R. Michaely, M. Richardson, and M. Roberts (2007), 'On the importance of measuring payout yield: Implications for empirical asset pricing'. *Journal of Finance* **62**, 877–915.

Bouwman, C., K. Fuller, and A. Nain (2009), 'The performance of stock-price driven acquisitions'. *Review of Financial Studies* **22**, 633–679.

Brav, A., J. Graham, C. Harvey, and R. Michaely (2005), 'Payout policy in the 21st century'. *Journal of Financial Economics* **77**, 483–527.

Brocas, I. and J. Carrillo (2008), 'The brain as a hierarchical organization'. *American Economic Review* **98**, 1312–1346.

Bruhin, A., H. Fehr-Duda, and T. Epper (2009a), 'Risk and rationality: Uncovering heterogeneity in probability distortion'. Working paper, ET: Zurich.

Bruhin, A., H. Fehr-Duda, and T. Epper (2009b), 'Uncertainty breeds decreasing impatience: The role of risk preferences in time discounting'. Working paper (ET: Zurich).

Brunnermeier, M., D. Diamond, and R. Rajam (2008), 'Deciphering the liquidity and credit crunch 2007–08'. NBER Working Paper No. 14612.

Burger, J. and H. Cooper (1979), 'The desirability of control'. *Motivation and Emotion* **3**, 381–393.

Cai, Y. and M. Sevilir (2009), 'Board connections and M&A transactions'. Working paper, University of North Carolina.

Camerer, C. (1995), 'Individual decision making'. In: J. Kagel and A. Roth (eds.): *The Handbook of Experimental Economics*. Princeton University Press, pp. 587–703.

Campbell, C., S. Johnson, J. Rutherford, and B. Stanley (2009), 'CEO confidence and forced turnover'. Working paper, Texas A&M University.

Campbell, J. (2000), 'Asset pricing at the millenium'. *Journal of Finance.*

Campbell, J. and R. Shiller (1991), 'Yield spreads and interest rate movements: A bird's eye view'. *Review of Economic Studies* **58**, 495–514.

Campbell, J. Y. and J. Cochrane (1999), 'By Force of Habit: A consumption-based explanation of aggregate stock market behavior'. *Journal of Political Economy* **107**, 205–251.

Chan, W. S., R. Frankel, and S. P. Kothari (2003), 'Testing behavioural finance theories using trends and sequences in financial performance'. Working paper (MIT).

Chen, J., H. Hong, and J. Stein (2002), 'Breadth of ownership and stock returns'. *Journal of Financial Economics* **66**, 171–205.

Chirinko, R. and H. Schaller (2001), 'Business fixed investment and 'bubbles': The Japanese case'. *American Economic Review* **91**, 663–680.

Chirinko, R. and H. Schaller (2004), 'Glamour vs. value: The real story'. Working paper, Emory University.

Chopra, N., J. Lakonishok, and J. Ritter (1992), 'Measuring abnormal performance: do stocks overreact?'. *Journal of Financial Economics* **31**, 235–268.

CNN, December 1, (2008), 'Government warned of mortgage meltdown: Regulators ignored warnings about risky mortgages, delayed regulations on the industry'.

Cochrane, J. (2000), *Asset Pricing.* Princeton: Princeton University Press, 1st edition.

Cochrane, J. (2005), *Asset Pricing.* Princeton: Princeton University Press, 2nd edition.

Cochrane, J. and M. Piazzesi (2005), 'Bond Risk Premia'. *American Economic Review* **95**, 138–160.

Constantinides, G. (1990), 'Habit formation: A resolution of the equity premium puzzle'. *Journal of Political Economy* **98**, 519–543.

Constantinides, G., J. Jackwerth, and S. Perrakis (2009), 'Mispricing of S&P 500 index options'. *Review of Financial Studies* **22**, 1247–1277.

Cooper, A., C. Woo, and W. Dunkelberg (1988), 'Entrepreneurs' perceived chances for success'. *Journal of Business Venturing* **3**, 97–108.

Cooper, M., O. Dimitrov, and P. R. Rau (2001), 'A rose.com by any other name'. *Journal of Finance* **56**, 2371–2388.

Coval, J. and T. Shumway (2005), 'Do behavioral biases affect prices?'. *Journal of Finance* **60**, 1–34.

Dai, Q. and K. Singleton (2003), 'Term structure dynamics in theory and reality'. *Review of Financial Studies* **16**, 631–678.

Daniel, K., D. Hirshleifer, and A. Subrahmanyam (1998), 'Investor psychology and security market under- and overreactions'. *Journal of Finance* **53**, 1839–1885.

Daniel, K., D. Hirshleifer, and A. Subrahmanyam (2001), 'Overconfidence, arbitrage and equilibrium asset pricing'. *Journal of Finance* **56**, 921–965.

Daniel, K. D. and S. Titman (2006), 'Market reactions to tangible and intangible information'. *Journal of Finance* **61**, 1605–1643.

De Bondt, W., H. Shefrin, G. Muradoglu, and S. Staikouras (2008), 'Behavioral finance: Quo vadis?'. *Journal of Applied Finance* **18**(2), 7–21.

De Giorgi, E. (2009), 'Goal-based investing with cumulative prospect theory and satisficing behavior'. Working paper, University of Lugano.

De Giorgi, E., T. Hens, and M. Rieger (2009), 'Financial market equilibria with cumulative prospect theory'. Working paper, University of Zurich.

DeBondt, W. and R. Thaler (1985), 'Does the stock market overreact?'. *Journal of Finance* **40**, 793–808.

Degeorge, F., F. Derrien, and K. Womack (2007), 'Analyst Hype in IPOs: Explaining the popularity of bookbuilding'. *Review of Financial Studies* **20**, 1021–1058.

DeLong, J. B., A. Shleifer, L. Summers, and R. Waldmann (1990a), 'Noise trader risk in financial markets'. *Journal of Political Economy* **98**, 703–738.

DeLong, J. B., A. Shleifer, L. Summers, and R. Waldmann (1990b), 'Positive feedback investment strategies and destabilizing rational speculation'. *Journal of Finance* **45**, 375–395.

DeLong, J. B., A. Shleifer, L. Summers, and R. Waldmann (1991), 'The survival of noise traders in financial markets'. *Journal of Business* **64**, 1–20.

Detemple, J. and S. Murthy (1994), 'Intertemporal asset pricing with heterogeneous beliefs'. *Journal of Economic Theory* **62**, 294–320.

Dichev, I. (2004), 'What are stock investors' actual historical returns?'. University of Michigan working paper.

Diecidue, E. and D. La-Ornual (2009), 'Reconciling support theory and the book-making principle'. *Journal of Risk and Uncertainty*, forthcoming.

Diecidue, E. and J. van de Ven (2008), 'Aspiration level, probability of success and failure, and expected utility'. *International Economic Review* **49**, 683–700.

Diener, E., R. Emmons, R. Larsen, and S. Griffin (1985), 'The satisfaction with life scale'. *Journal of Personality Assessment* **49**, 71–75.

Diether, K., C. Malloy, and A. Scherbina (2004), 'Differences of opinion and the cross-section of stock returns'. *Journal of Finance* **57**, 2113–2141.

Dittmar, R. (2002), 'Nonlinear pricing kernels, kurtosis preference, and evidence from the cross section of equity returns'. *Journal of Finance* **57**, 369–403.

Dong, M., D. Hirshleifer, S. Richardson, and S. Teoh (2003), 'Does investor misvaluation drive the takeover market?'. *Journal of Finance* **61**, 725–762.

Dong, M., C. Robinson, and C. Veld (2005), 'Why individual investors want dividends'. *Journal of Corporate Finance* **12**, 121–158.

Dorn, D. and G. Huberman (2005), 'Talk and action: What individual investors say and what they do'. *Review of Finance* **9**, 437–481.

Doukas, J. A. and P. J. McKnight (2005), 'European momentum strategies, information diffusion, and investor conservatism'. *European Financial Management* **11**, 313–338.

Doukas, J. A. and D. Petmezas (2005), 'Acquisitions, overconfident managers and self-attribution bias'. Working Paper, Old Dominion University.

Duffie, D., L. Saita, and K. Wang (2007), 'Multi-period corporate default prediction with stochastic variates'. *Journal of Financial Economics* **83**, 635–665.

Dumas, B., A. Kurshev, and R. Uppal (2009), 'What can rational investors do about excessive volatility and sentiment fluctuations?'. *Journal of Finance*, forthcoming.

Edmans, A., D. Garcia, and O. Norli (2007), 'Sports sentiment and stock returns'. *Journal of Finance* **62**, 1967–1998.

Edwards, W. (1968), 'Conservatism in human information processing'. In: B. Kleinmutz (ed.): *Formal Representation of Human Judgement*. New York: Wiley.

Fama, E. and K. French (1993), 'Common risk factors in the returns of bonds and stocks'. *Journal of Financial Economics* **33**, 3–56.

Fama, E. and K. French (1995), 'Size and book-to-market factors in earnings and returns'. *Journal of Finance* **50**, 131–155.

Fama, E. and K. French (1996), 'Multifactor explanations of asset pricing anomalies'. *Journal of Finance* **51**, 55–84.

Fama, E. and K. French (2001), 'Disappearing dividends: Changing firm characteristics or lower propensity to pay?'. *Journal of Financial Economics* **60**, 3–43.

Feng, L. and M. Seasholes (2005), 'Do investor sophistication and trading experience eliminate behavioral biases in finance markets?'. *Review of Finance* **9**, 305–351.

Flynn, J., P. Slovic, and C. K. Mertz (1994), 'Gender, race, and the perception of environmental health risks'. *Risk Analysis* **14**, 1101–1198.

Fogel, S. and T. Berry (2006), 'The disposition effect and individual investor decisions: The roles of regret and counterfactual alternatives'. *Journal of Behavioral Finance* **7**, 107–116.

Foldes, L. (1978), 'Martingale conditions for optimal saving: Discrete time'. *Journal of Mathematical Economics* **5**, 83–96.

Foldes, L. (2000), 'Valuation and martingale properties of shadow prices: An exposition'. *Journal of Economic Dynamics and Control* **24**, 1641–1701.

Fox, C. and K. See (2003), 'Belief and preference in decision under uncertainty'. In: D. Hardman and L. Macchi (eds.): *Thinking: Psychological Perspectives on Reasoning, Judgment and Decision Making*. John Wiley and Sons.

Fracassi, C. and G. Tate (2009), 'External networking and internal firm governance'. Working paper (UCLA).

French, K. and J. Poterba (1991), 'Investor diversification and international equity markets'. *American Economic Review* **81**, 222–226.

Frieder, L. (2004), 'Earnings announcements, order flow, and returns'. Working Paper, Purdue University.

Frieder, L. and A. Subrahmanyam (2005), 'Brand perceptions and the market for common stock'. *Journal of Financial and Quantitative Analysis* **40**, 57–85.

Froot, K. and E. Dabora (1999), 'How are stock prices affected by the location of trade?'. *Journal of Financial Economics* **53**, 189–216.

Gaston-Breton, C. and J. Lejarraga (2009), 'Biases in learning from past strategic decisions'. Working paper, Universidad Carlos III de Madrid.

Genesove, D. and C. Mayer (2001), 'Loss aversion and seller behavior: Evidence from the housing market'. *Quarterly Journal of Economics* **116**, 1233–1260.

Gentry, W. and G. Hubbard (2001), 'Entrepreneurship and household saving'. NBER Working Paper No. 7894.

Gervais, S., J. B. Heaton, and T. Odean (2003), 'Overconfidence, investment policy, and executive stock options'. Working paper, Duke University.

Gilchrist, S., C. Himmelberg, and G. Huberman (2004), 'Do stock price bubbles influence corporate investment?'. *Journal of Monetary Economics* **52**, 805–827.

Goel, A. and A. Thakor (2008), 'Overconfidence, CEO selection, and corporate governance'. *Journal of Finance* **63**, 2737–2784.

Goetzmann, W. and N. Zhu (2005), 'Rain or shine: Where is the weather effect?'. *European Financial Management* **11**, 559–578.

Goetzmann, W. N. and A. Kumar (2008), 'Equity portfolio diversification'. *Review of Finance* **12**, 433–463.

Gollier, C. and B. Salanié (2006), 'Individual decisions under risk, risk sharing and asset prices with regret'. Working paper (University of Toulouse).

Gompers, P., J. Ishii, and A. Metrick (2003), 'Corporate governance and equity prices'. *Quarterly Journal of Economics* **118**, 107–155.

Graham, J. and C. Harvey (2001), 'The theory and practice of corporate finance: Evidence from the field'. *Journal of Financial Economics* **60**, 187–243.

Graham, J., C. Harvey, and M. Puri (2009), 'Managerial attitudes and corporate actions'. Working Paper, Duke University.

Graham, J., C. Harvey, and S. Rajgopal (2004), 'The economic implications of corporate financial reporting'. *Journal of Accounting and Economics* **40**, 3–73.

Graham, J. and A. Kumar (2006), 'Dividend preference of retail investors: Do dividend clienteles exist?'. *Journal of Finance* **6**, 1305 1336.

Graham, J. R. (2000), 'How big are the tax benefits of debt?'. *Journal of Finance* **55**, 1901–1941.

Griffin, D. and A. Tversky (1992), 'The weighing of evidence and the determinants of overconfidence'. *Cognitive Psychology* **24**, 411–435.

Griffin, J. and D. Tang (2009), 'Did subjectivity play a role in CDO credit ratings?'. Working paper, University of Texas.

Grinblatt, M. and B. Han (2004), 'Prospect theory, mental accounting and momentum'. *Journal of Financial Economics* **78**, 311–333.

Grinblatt, M. and M. Keloharju (2001a), 'How distance, language, and culture influence stockholdings and trades'. *Journal of Finance* **56**, 1053–1073.

Grinblatt, M. and M. Keloharju (2001b), 'What makes investors trade?'. *Journal of Finance* **56**, 589–616.

Grinblatt, M. and M. Keloharju (2009), 'Sensation seeking, overconfidence, and trading activity'. *Journal of Finance* **64**, 549–578.

Guedes, J. and T. Opler (1996), 'The determinants of the maturity of corporate debt issues'. *Journal of Finance* **51**, 1809–1833.

Guedj, I. and D. Scharfstein (2004), 'Organizational scope and investment: Evidence from the drug development strategies of biopharmaceutical firms'. NBER Working Paper No. w10933.

Gurkaynak, R., B. Sack, and E. Swanson (2005), 'The excess sensitivity of long-term interest rates: Evidence and implications for macroeconomic models'. *American Economic Review* **95**, 425–436.

Hackbarth, D. (2009), 'Determinants of corporate borrowing: A behavioral perspective'. *Journal of Corporate Finance* **15**, 389–411.

Hamilton, B. (2000), 'Does entrepreneurship pay? An empirical analysis of the returns to self-employment'. *Journal of Political Economy* **108**, 604–631.

Han, B. (2008), 'Investor sentiment and option prices'. *Review of Financial Studies* **21**, 387–414.

Hansen, L. P. and R. Jagannathan (1991), 'Implications of security market data for models of dynamic economies'. *Journal of Political Economy* **99**, 225–262.

Hare, T., C. Camerer, and A. Rangel (2009), 'Self-control in decision-making involves modulation of the vmPFC valuation system'. *Science* **324**, 646–648.

Harrison, J. M. and D. Kreps (1978), 'Speculative investor behavior in a stock market with heterogeneous expectations'. *Quarterly Journal of Economics* **92**, 323–336.

Harvey, C. and A. Siddique (2000), 'Conditional skewness in asset pricing tests'. *Journal of Finance* **55**, 1263–1295.

Haugen, R. A. and N. L. Baker (1996), 'Commonality in the determinants of expected stock returns'. *Journal of Financial Economics* **41**, 401–439.

He, X. and X. Zhou (2009), 'Behavioral portfolio choice: an analytical treatment'. Working paper, Oxford University.

Heath, C., R. Larrick, and J. Klayman (1998), 'Cognitive repairs: How organizational practices can compensate for individual shortcomings'. *Research in Organizational Behavior* **20**, 1–37.

Heaton, J. and D. Lucas (2000), 'Asset pricing and portfolio choice: The importance of entrepreneurial risk'. *Journal of Finance* **55**, 1163–1198.

Heaton, J. B. (2002), 'Managerial optimism and corporate finance'. *Financial Management* **31**, 33–45.

Henderson, B., N. Jegadeesh, and M. Weisbach (2009), 'World markets for raising new capital'. *Journal of Financial Economics* **82**, 63–101.

Hens, T. and K. Schenk-Hoppé (2008), *Handbook of Financial Markets: Dynamics and Evolution*. Amsterdam: Elsevier.

Hens, T. and M. Vlcek (2005), 'Does prospect theory explain the disposition effect?'. Working paper, University of Zurich.

Hirshleifer, D. (2008a), 'Investor psychology and asset pricing'. *Journal of Finance* **56**, 1533–1598.

Hirshleifer, D. (2008b), 'Psychological bias as a driver of financial regulation'. *European Financial Management* **14**, 856–874.

Hirshleifer, D. and T. Shumway (2003), 'Good day sunshine: Stock returns and the weather'. *Journal of Finance* **58**, 1009–1032.

Hirshleifer, D., A. Subrahmanyam, and S. Titman (2006), 'Feedback and the success of irrational traders'. *Journal of Financial Economics* **81**, 311–388.

Hoffmann, A., H. Shefrin, and J. Pennings (2010), 'Behavioral portfolio analysis of individual investors'. Working Paper, Maastricht University and Netspar.

Hong, H., T. Lim, and J. Stein (2000), 'Bad news travels slowly: Size, analyst coverage, and the profitability of momentum strategies'. *Journal of Finance* **55**, 265–295.

Hong, H. and J. Stein (1999), 'A unified theory of underreaction, momentum trading, and overreaction in asset markets'. *Journal of Finance* **54**, 2143–2184.

Hong, H. and J. Stein (2003), 'Differences of opinion, short-sale constraints and market crashes'. *Review of Financial Studies* **16**, 487–525.

Hong, H. G., J. C. Stein, and J. Yu (2007), 'Simple forecasts and paradigm shifts'. *Journal of Finance* **62**, 1207–1242.

Hovakimian, A. (2006), 'Are observed capital structures determined by equity market timing?'. *Journal of Financial and Quantitative Analysis* **41**, 221–243.

Huang, R. and J. Ritter (2009), 'Testing theories of capital structure and estimating the speed of adjustment'. *Journal of Financial and Quantitative Analysis* **44**, 237–271.

Huberman, G. (2001), 'Familiarity breeds investment'. *Review of Financial Studies* **14**, 659–680.

Huddart, S., M. Lang, and M. Yetman (2009), 'Volume and price patterns around a stock's 52-week highs and lows: Theory and evidence'. *Management Science* **55**, 16–31.

Hvidkjaer, S. (2005), 'Small trades and the cross-section of stock returns'. Working paper, University of Maryland.

Hvidkjaer, S. (2006), 'A trade-based analysis of momentum'. *Review of Financial Studies* **19**, 457–491.

Ikenberry, D., J. Lakonishok, and T. Vermaelen (1995), 'Market underreaction to open market share repurchases'. *Journal of Financial Economics* **39**, 181–208.

Ikenberry, D., J. Lakonishok, and T. Vermaelen (2000), 'Stock repurchases in Canada: Performance and strategic trading'. *Journal of Finance* **55**, 2373–2398.

Ingersoll, J. (2008), 'Non-Monotonicity of the Tversky-Kahneman probability weighting function: A cautionary note'. *European Financial Management* **14**, 385–390.

Ishii, J. and Y. Xuan (2009), 'Acquirer-target social ties and merger outcomes'. Working Paper, Stanford University.

Jackwerth, J. C. (2000), 'Recovering risk aversion from options prices and realized returns'. *Review of Financial Studies* **13**, 433–451.

Janis, I. (1972), *Victims of Groupthink: A Psychological Study of Foreign Policy Decisions and Fiascoes.* Houghton Mifflin.

Jenter, D. (2005), 'Market timing and managerial portfolio decisions'. *Journal of Finance* **60**, 1903–1949.

Jones, C. and O. Lamont (2002), 'Short-sale constraints and stock returns'. *Journal of Financial Economics* **66**, 207–239.

Jouini, E. and C. Napp (2006), 'Heterogeneous beliefs and asset pricing in discrete time'. *Journal of Economic Dynamics and Control* **30**, 1233–1260.

Jouini, E. and C. Napp (2007), 'Consensus consumer and intertemporal asset pricing with heterogeneous beliefs'. *Review of Economic Studies* **74**, 1149–1174.

Kahneman, D., J. Knetsch, and R. Thaler (1991), 'Fairness as a constraint on profit seeking entitlements in the market'. In: R. Thaler (ed.): *Quasi-Rational Economics.* New York: Russell Sage Foundation.

Kahneman, D., P. Slovic, and A. Tversky (1982), *Judgment Under Uncertainty: Heuristics and Biases*. Cambridge: Cambridge University Press.

Kahneman, D. and A. Tversky (1973), 'On the psychology of prediction'. *Psychological Review* **80**, 237–251.

Kahneman, D. and A. Tversky (1979), 'Prospect theory: An analysis of decision making under risk'. *Econometrica* pp. 263–291.

Kahneman, D. and A. Tversky (1982), 'The psychology of preferences'. *Scientific American* **246**, 160–173.

Kamstra, M., L. Kramer, M. Levi, and T. Wang (2009), 'Time-varying preferences and SAD: Evidence from an asset pricing model'. Working paper, University of Toronto.

Kamstra, M. J., L. A. Kramer, and M. D. Levi (2000), 'Losing sleep at the market: The daylight-savings anomaly'. *American Economic Review* **90**, 1005 1011.

Kausar, A. and R. Taffler (2006), 'Testing behavioural finance models of market under and overreaction: Do they really work?'. Working Paper (University of Edinburgh.

Kaustia, M. (2004), 'Market-wide impact of the disposition effect: Evidence from IPO trading volume'. *Journal of Financial Markets* **7**, 207–235.

Kaustia, M. (2009), 'Prospect theory and the disposition effect'. *Journal of Financial and Quantitative Analysis*, forthcoming.

Kaustia, M. and S. Knüpfer (2009), 'Learning from the outcomes of others: Evidence from the stock market'. Working paper, Aalto University.

Klayman, J. and Y. Ha (1987), 'Confirmation, disconfirmation and information in hypothesis testing'. *Psychological Review* **94**, 211–228.

Klein, P. (2001), 'Were the acquisitive conglomerates inefficient?'. *RAND Journal of Economics* **32**, 745–761.

Knoch, D., F. Schneiderb, D. Schunk, M. Hohmann, and E. Fehr (2009), 'Disrupting the prefrontal cortex diminishes the human ability to build a good reputation'. *PNAS* **106**, 20895–20899.

Knutson, B. and C. Kuhnen (2009), 'The impact of affect on beliefs, preferences and financial decisions'. *Journal of Financial and Quantitative Analysis*, forthcoming.

Knutson, B., C. Kuhnen, G. E. Wimmer, and P. Winkielman (2008), 'Nucleus accumbens activation mediates the influence of reward cues on financial risk-taking'. *NeuroReport* **19**, 509–513.

Kräussl, R., A. Lucas, D. Rijsbergen, P. van der Sluis, and E. Vrugt (2009), 'Washington meets wall street: A closer examination of the presidential cycle puzzle'. Working paper, University of Amsterdam.

Kumar, A. (2009), 'Who gambles in the stock market?'. *Journal of Finance* **64**, 1889–1933.

Kuran, T. and C. Sunstein (1999), 'Availability cascades and risk regulation'. *Stanford Law Review* **51**, 683–768.

Kurz, M. (1997), *Endogenous Economic Fluctuations: Studies in the Theory of Rational Beliefs*. Studies in Economic Theory No. 6, Springer-Verlag: Berlin and New York.

Kyle, A. and F. A. Wang (1997), 'Speculation duopoly with agreement to disagree: Can overconfidence survive the market test?'. *Journal of Finance* **52**, 2073–2090.

La Porta, R., J. Lakonishok, A. Shleifer, and R. Vishny (1997), 'Good news for value stocks: further evidence on market efficiency'. *Journal of Finance* **49**, 1541–1578.

Lakonishok, J., I. Lee, N. Pearson, and A. Poteshman (2007), 'Option market activity'. *The Review of Financial Studies* **20**, 813–857.

Lakonishok, J., A. Shleifer, and R. W. Vishny (1994), 'Contrarian investment, extrapolation and risk'. *Journal of Finance* **49**, 1541–1578.

Lamont, O. (2000), 'Investment plans and stock returns'. *Journal of Finance* **55**, 2719–2745.

Landier, A. and D. Thesmar (2009), 'Financial contracting with optimistic entrepreneurs: Theory and evidence'. *Review of Financial Studies* **22**, 117–150.

Leary, M. (1983), 'Social anxiousness: The construct and its measurement'. *Journal of Personality Assessment* **47**(1), 66–75.

Lee, C., A. Shleifer, and R. Thaler (1991), 'Investor sentiment and the closed-end fund puzzle'. *Journal of Finance* **46**, 75–110.

Lehenkari, M. (2008), 'The disposition effect: Underlying mechanisms and implications for individual investors'. Working paper, University of Oulu, Finland.

Lennox, R. and R. Wolfe (1984), 'Revision of the self-monitoring scale'. *Journal of Personality and Social Psychology* **46**, 1349–1364.

LeRoy, S. and R. Porter (1981), 'The present-value relation: Tests based on implied variance bounds'. *Econometrica* **49**, 97–113.

Lintner, J. (1969), 'The aggregation of investors' diverse judgments and preferences in pure competitive markets'. *Journal of Financial and Quantitative Analysis* **4**, 347–400.

Lobe, S. and A. Hölzl (2008), 'Happy savers, happy issuer: The UK lottery bond'. Center of Finance, University of Regensburg, Forthcoming *Revue Bancaire et Financière - Bank- en Financiewezen J.E.*

Loomes, G. and R. Sugden (1982), 'Regret theory: An alternative theory of rational choice under uncertainty'. *Economic Journal* **92**, 805–824.

Lopes, L. (1987), 'Between hope and fear: The psychology of risk'. *Advances in Experimental Social Psychology* **20**, 255–295.

Lopes, L. L. and G. C. Oden (1999), 'The role of aspiration level in risk choice: A comparison of cumulative prospect theory and SP/A theory'. *Journal of Mathematical Psychology* **43**, 286–313.

Loughran, T. and J. Ritter (1995), 'The new issues puzzle'. *Journal of Finance* **50**, 23–51.

Loughran, T. and J. Ritter (2002), 'Why don't issuers get upset about leaving money on the table in IPOs?'. *Review of Financial Studies* **15**, 413–443.

Loughran, T., J. Ritter, and K. Rydqvist (1994), 'Initial public offerings: International insights'. *Pacific-Basin Finance Journal* **2**, 165–199.

Loughran, T. and A. Vijh (1997), 'Do long-term shareholders benefit from corporate acquisitions?'. *Journal of Finance* **52**, 1765–1790.

Malmendier, U. and G. Tate (2005), 'CEO overconfidence and corporate investment'. *Journal of Finance* **60**, 2661–2700.

Malmendier, U. and G. Tate (2008), 'Who makes acquisitions? CEO overconfidence and the market's reaction'. *Journal of Financial Economics* **89**, 20–43.

Marsh, P. (1982), 'The choice between equity and debt: An empirical study'. *Journal of Finance* **37**, 121–144.

McConnell, J. and E. Schwartz (1992), 'The origin of LYONs: A case study in financial innovation'. *Journal of Applied Corporate Finance* pp. 40–47.

Mehra, R. and E. Prescott (1985), 'The equity premium: A puzzle'. *Journal of Monetary Economics* **15**, 145–161.

Merrow, E., K. Phillips, and C. Myers (1981), *Understanding Cost Growth and Performance Shortfalls in Pioneer Process Plants.* Santa Monica, CA: Rand.

Merton, R. C. (1971), 'Optimum consumption and portfolio rules in a continuous-time model'. *Journal of Economic Theory* **3**, 373–413.

Miller, E. (1977), 'Risk, uncertainty, and divergence of opinion'. *Journal of Finance* **32**, 1151–1168.

Mitchell, O., G. Mottola, S. Utkus, and T. Yamaguchi (2006), 'The inattentive participant: Portfolio trading behavior in 401(k) plans'. Working Paper, Wharton.

Moskowitz, T. and A. Vissing-Jorgensen (2002), 'The returns to entrepreneurial investment: A private equity premium puzzle?'. *American Economic Review* **92**, 745–778.

Muelbroek, L. (1992), 'An empirical analysis of illegal insider trading'. *Journal of Finance* **47**, 1661–1699.

Nagel, S. (2005), 'Short sales institutional investors and the cross-section of stock returns'. *Journal of Financial Economics* **78**, 277–309.

Odean, T. (1998a), 'Are investors reluctant to realize their losses?'. *Journal of Finance* **53**, 1775–1798.

Odean, T. (1998b), 'Volume, volatility, price, and profit when all traders are above average'. *Journal of Finance* **53**, 1887–1934.

Odean, T. (1999), 'Do investors trade too much?'. *American Economic Review* **89**, 1279–1298.

Panageas, S. (2003), 'Speculation, overpricing, and investment: Theory and empirical evidence'. Working Paper, MIT.

Payne, J. (2005), 'It is whether you win or lose: The importance of the overall probabilities of winning or losing in risky choice'. *The Journal of Risk and Uncertainty* **30**, 5–19.

PBS (2009), 'The warning'. Frontline television documentary.

Peltzman, S. (1976), 'Toward a more general theory of regulation'. *Journal of Law and Economics* **19**, 211–240.

Peyer, U. and T. Vermaelen (2009), 'The nature and persistence of buyback anomalies'. *Review of Financial Studies* **22**, 1693–1745.

Polk, C. and P. Sapienza (2004), 'The real effects of investor sentiment'. NBER working paper no. 10563.

Polkovnichenko, V. (2002), 'Household portfolio diversification: A case for rank-dependent preferences'. *Review of Financial Studies* **18**, 1467–1501.

Posner, R. A. (2009), *A Failure of Capitalism: The Crisis of '08 and the Descent into Depression.* Cambridge, MA: Harvard University Press.

Poteshman, A. (2001), 'Underreaction, overreaction and increasing misreaction to information in the options market'. *Journal of Finance* **56**, 851–876.

Poteshman, A. and V. Serbin (2003), 'Clearly irrational financial market behavior: Evidence from the early exercise of exchange traded stock options'. *Journal of Finance* **58**, 37–70.

Poti, V. (2006), 'The coskewness puzzle in the cross-section of industry portfolio returns'. Working paper, Dublin City University Business School.

Puri, M. and D. Robinson (2007), 'Optimism and economic choice'. *Journal of Financial Economics* **86**, 71–99.

Puri, M. and D. Robinson (2008), 'Who are entrepreneurs and why do they behave that way?'. Working Paper, Duke University.

Rather, D. (2009), 'Sold!'. Dan Rather Reports, Episode Number: 407, February 17.

Rau, P. and T. Vermaelen (1998), 'Glamour, value and the post-acquisition performance of acquiring firms'. *Journal of Financial Economics* **49**, 223–253.

Ravenscraft, D. and F. Scherer (1987), *Mergers, Sell-Offs, and Economic Efficiency.* Washington, DC: Brookings Institution.

Richardson, S. and R. Sloan (2003), 'External financing and future stock returns'. Working paper, University of Pennsylvania.

Rieger, M. (2008), 'Probability misestimation and preferences in financial investment decision'. Working Paper, University of Zurich.

Roll, R. (1986), 'The hubris hypothesis of corporate takeovers'. *Journal of Business* **59**, 197–216.

Rosenberg, J. and R. Engle (2004), 'Empirical pricing kernels'. *Journal of Financial Economics* **64**, 341–372.

Ross, L., D. Green, and P. House (1977), 'The 'false consensus effect': An egocentric bias in social perception and attribution processes'. *Journal of Experimental Social Psychology* **13**, 279–301.

Ross, S. (2005), *Neoclassical Finance.* Princeton, NJ: Princeton University Press.

Samuelson, W. and R. Zeckhauser (1988), 'Status quo bias in decision making'. *Journal of Risk and Uncertainty* **1**, 7–59.

Saunders, E. M. J. (1993), 'Stock prices and Wall Street weather'. *American Economic Review* **83**, 1337–1345.

Scarpetta, S., P. Hemmings, T. Tressel, and J. Woo (2002), 'The role of policy and institutions for productivity and firm dynamics: Evidence from micro and industry data'. OECD working paper.

Scheier, M. F. and C. S. Carver (1985), 'Optimism, coping and health: Assessment and implications of generalized outcome expectancies'. *Health Psychology* **4**, 219–247.

Scheinkman, J. and W. Xiong (2003), 'Overconfidence and speculative bubbles'. *Journal of Political Economy* **111**, 1183–1219.

Seru, A., T. Shumway, and N. Stoffman (2009), 'Learning by trading'. *Review of Financial Studies*, forthcoming.

Seyhun, H. N. (1992), 'Why does aggregate insider trading predict future stock returns?'. *The Quarterly Journal of Economics* **107**, 1303–1331.

Shefrin, H. (2001), 'Behavioral corporate finance'. *Journal of Applied Corporate Finance* **14**, 113–124.

Shefrin, H. (2005), *Behavioral Corporate Finance.* Burr Ridge: McGraw-Hill.

Shefrin, H. (2007), 'Behavioral portfolio selection'. In: *Encyclopedia of Quantitative Finance.* Wiley, forthcoming.

Shefrin, H. (2008a), *A Behavioral Approach to Asset Pricing.* Boston: Elsevier Academic Press, 2nd edition.

Shefrin, H. (2008b), 'Behavioral explanations for why individual investors find dividends attractive'. In: H. K. Baker (ed.):

Chapter 13, *the Blackwell Companion to Dividends and Dividend Policy*. Blackwell.

Shefrin, H. (2008c), 'Risk and return in behavioral SDF-based asset pricing models'. *Journal of Investment Management* **6**, 4–22.

Shefrin, H. (2009), 'How psychological pitfalls generated the global financial crisis'. In: L. Siegel (ed.): *Understanding the Global Financial Crisis*.

Shefrin, H. (2010), 'Insights into the psychological profiles of entrepreneurs'. In: R. Yazdipour (ed.): *Advances in Entrepreneurial Finance*. New York, NY: Springer, forthcoming.

Shefrin, H. and M. Statman (1984), 'Explaining investor preference for cash dividends'. *Journal of Financial Economics* **13**, 253–282.

Shefrin, H. and M. Statman (1985), 'The disposition to sell winners too early and ride losers too long: theory and evidence'. *Journal of Finance* **40**, 777–790.

Shefrin, H. and M. Statman (1992), *Ethics, Fairness, Efficiency, and Financial Markets*. Charlottesville, VA: CFA Institute Publications.

Shefrin, H. and M. Statman (1993a), 'Behavioral aspects of the design and marketing of financial products'. *Financial Management* **22**, 123–134.

Shefrin, H. and M. Statman (1993b), 'Ethics, fairness and efficiency in financial markets'. *Financial Analysts Journal* pp. 21–29.

Shefrin, H. and M. Statman (1994), 'Behavioral capital asset pricing theory'. *Journal of Financial and Quantitative Analysis* **29**, 323–349.

Shefrin, H. and M. Statman (2000), 'Behavioral portfolio theory'. *Journal of Financial and Quantitative Analysis* **35**, 127–151.

Shefrin, H. and M. Statman (2009), 'Striking regulatory irons while hot'. *Journal of Investment Management* **7**, 29–42.

Shefrin, H. and R. Thaler (1988), 'The behavioral life cycle hypothesis'. *Economic Inquiry* **24**, 609–643.

Shiller, R. (1978), 'The volatility of long-term interest rates and the expectations models of the term structure'. *Journal of Political Economy* **87**, 1190–1219.

Shiller, R. (1981), 'Do stock prices move too much to be justified by subsequent changes in dividends?'. *American Economic Review* **71**, 421–436.

Shiller, R. (1999), 'Human behavior and the efficiency of the financial system'. In: J. Taylor and M. Woodford (eds.): *Handbook of Macroeconomics*. Amsterdam: Elsevier.

Shiller, R. (2005), *Irrational Exuberance*. Princeton: Princeton University Press.

Shiller, R. and J. Pound (1989), 'Survey evidence on the diffusion of interest and information among investors'. *Journal of Economic Behavior and Organization* **12**, 46–66.

Shleifer, A. (2000), *Inefficient Markets*. Oxford: Oxford University Press.

Shleifer, A. and R. Vishny (2003), 'Stock market driven acquisitions'. *Journal of Financial Economics* **70**, 295–312.

Sloan, R. (1996), 'Do stock prices fully reflect information in accruals and cash flows about future earnings?'. *The Accounting Review* **71**, 289–316.

Slovic, P. (1972), 'Psychological study of human judgment: Implications for investment decision making'. *Journal of Finance* **27**, 779–799.

Smith, V. (2003), 'Constructivist and ecological rationality in economics'. *American Economic Review* **93**, 465–507.

Snyder, M. (1974), 'Self-monitoring of expressive behavior'. *Journal of Personality and Social Psychology* **30**, 526–537.

Sorescu, S. and A. Subrahmanyam (2006), 'The cross section of analyst recommendations'. *Journal of Financial and Quantitative Analysis* **41**, 139–168.

Spalt, O. (2008), 'Probability weighting and employee stock options'. Working paper, University of Mannheim.

Stasser, G., L. Taylor, and C. Hanna (1989), 'Information sampling in structured and unstructured discussions of three- and six-person groups'. *Journal of Personality and Social Psychology* **57**, 67–78.

Stasser, G. and W. Titus (1985), 'Pooling of unshared information in group decision making: Biased information sampling during discussion'. *Journal of Personality and Social Psychology* **48**, 1467–1478.

Statman, M. (2002), 'Lottery players: Stock traders'. *Financial Analysts Journal* **58**, 14–21.

Statman, M. (2008), 'The expressive nature of socially responsible investors'. *Journal of Financial Planning* pp. 40–46.

Statman, M. (2009), 'Regulating financial markets: Protecting us from ourselves and others'. *Financial Analysts Journal* **65**, 22–31.

Statman, M. and D. Caldwell (1987), 'Applying behavioral finance to capital budgeting: Project termination'. *Financial Management* pp. 7–15.

Statman, M. and J. Sepe (1989), 'Project termination announcements and the market value of the firm'. *Financial Management* pp. 1–8.

Statman, M., S. Thorley, and K. Vorkink (2006), 'Investor overconfidence and trading volume'. *Review of Financial Studies* **19**, 1531–1565.

Statman, M. and T. Tyebjee (1985), 'Optimistic capital budgeting forecasts: An experiment'. *Financial Management* pp. 27–33.

Stein, J. (1989), 'Overreactions in the options market'. *Journal of Finance* **44**, 1011–1022.

Stein, J. (1996), 'Rational capital budgeting in an irrational world'. *Journal of Business* **69**, 429–455.

Stigler, G. (1971), 'The theory of economic regulation'. *The Bell Journal of Economics and Management Science* **2**, 3–21.

Subrahmanyam, A. (2007), 'Behavioural finance: A review and synthesis'. *European Financial Management* **14**(1), 12–29.

Sullivan, R. (2009), 'Governance: Travel and destinations'. *Financial Analysts Journal* **65**, 6–10.

Taleb, N. (2007), *The Black Swan.* New York: Random House.

Taylor, J. (2009), 'The financial crisis and the policy responses: An empirical analysis of what went wrong'. NBER Working Paper No. 14631.

Teoh, S. H., I. Welch, and T. J. Wong (1998a), 'Earnings management and the long-run market performance of initial public offerings'. *Journal of Finance* **53**, 1935–1974.

Teoh, S. H., I. Welch, and T. J. Wong (1998b), 'Earnings management and the underperformance of seasoned equity offerings'. *Journal of Financial Economics* **50**, 63–99.

Thaler, R. (1993), *Advances in Behavioral Finance: Volume I.* New York: Russell Sage Foundation.

Thaler, R. and E. Johnson (1990), 'Gambling with the house money and trying to break even: The effects of prior outcomes on risky choice'. *Management Science* **36**, 643–660.

Titman, S., K. C. J. Wei, and F. Xie (2004), 'Capital investments and stock returns'. *Journal of Financial and Quantitative Analysis, International Review of Finance* **9**, 111–131.

Tiwana, A., J. Wang, M. Keil, and P. Ahluwalia (2007), 'The bounded rationality bias in managerial valuation of real options: Theory and evidence from IT projects'. *Decision Sciences* **38**, 157–181.

Todd, P. and G. Gigerenzer (2000), 'Simple heuristics that make us smart'. *Behavioral and Brain Sciences* **23**, 727–780.

Trivers, R. (1985), *Social Evolution.* Benjamin/Cummings, Menlo Park.

Trivers, R. (1991), 'Deceit and Self-deception'. In: R. Robinson and L. Tiger (eds.): *Man and Beast Revisited.* Washington D.C.: Smithsonian Press.

Tversky, A. and D. Kahneman (1992), 'Advances in prospect theory: Cumulative representation of uncertainty'. *Journal of Risk and Uncertainty* **5**, 297–323.

Tversky, A. and D. J. Koehler (1994), 'Support theory: A nonextensional representation of subjective probability'. *Psychological Review* **101**, 547–567.

Wadhwa, V., R. Aggarwal, K. Holly, and A. Salkever (2009), *The Anatomy of an Entrepreneur Family Background and Motivation.* Ewing Marion Kauffman Foundation of Entrepreneurship.

Wang, M., M. Rieger, and T. Hens (2009), 'International test on risk attitudes'. Working paper, University of Zurich.

Watson, D. and L. Clark (1988), 'Development and validation of brief measures of positive and negative affect: The PANAS scales'. *Journal of Personality and Social Psychology* **54**, 1063–1070.

Weinstein, N. (1980), 'Unrealistic optimism about future life events'. *Journal of Personality and Social Psychology* **39**, 806–820.

Welch, I. (2000), 'Views of financial economists on the equity premium and on professional controversies'. *Journal of Business* **73**, 501–537.

Xiong, W. and H. Yan (2009), 'Heterogeneous expectations and bond markets'. *Review of Financial Studies*, forthcoming.

Zhang, X. F. (2006), 'Information uncertainty and analyst forecast behavior'. *Journal of Finance* **61**, 105–136.

Lightning Source UK Ltd.
Milton Keynes UK
UKHW02f2350180618
324449UK00003B/220/P

9 781601 983305